BLONDIE

All The Top 40 Hits

Craig Halstead

Copyright © Craig Halstead 2022

All rights reserved. No part of this publication may be reproduced, stored in a retrieval system, or transmitted in any form or by any means, electronic, mechanical, photocopy, recording or otherwise, without prior written permission of the copyright owner. Nor can it be circulated in any form of binding or cover other than that in which it is published and without similar condition including this condition being imposed on a subsequent purchaser.

Second Edition

for Aaron

BY THE SAME AUTHOR ...

Christmas Number Ones

This book details the Christmas No.1 singles in the UK from 1940 to date, and also reveals the Christmas No.2 single and Christmas No.1 album. The book also features the Christmas No.1s in five other countries, namely Australia, Germany, Ireland, the Netherlands and the United States, and is up-dated annually in January.

The '*All The Top 40 Hits*' Series

This series documents, in chronological order, all the Top 40 Hit Singles and Albums by the featured artist:

ABBA
Annie Lennox (incl. Eurythmics)
Bee Gees
Blondie
Boney M.
Boy George & Culture Club
Carpenters
Chi-Lites & Stylistics
Donna Summer
George Michael (incl. Wham!)
Janet Jackson
Kate Bush
Kim Wilde
Lionel Richie (incl. Commodores)
Marvin Gaye
Michael Jackson
The Jacksons (Jackson 5 / Jacksons / Jermaine / La Toya / Rebbie / 3T)
Olivia Newton-John
Sam Cooke & Otis Redding
Dame Shirley Bassey
Slade
Spice Girls
Tina Turner
Whitney Houston

The '*For The Record*' Series

The books in this series are more comprehensive than the 'All The Top 40 Hits' volumes, and typically include: The Songs (released & unreleased), The Albums, The Home Videos, The TV Shows/Films, The Concerts, Chartography & USA/UK Chart Runs, USA Discography & UK Discography.

Donna Summer
Janet Jackson
Michael Jackson
Whitney Houston

Fiction

The James Harris Trilogy

The Secret Library
Shadow Of Death
Twist Of Fate

Cataclysm

Book 1: The First 73 Days
Book 2: A New Year

Stand Alone Novel

Tyranny

Novellas

Alone
Passion
Taboo

THE FEELIES · FRANCE GALL · YO LA TENGO

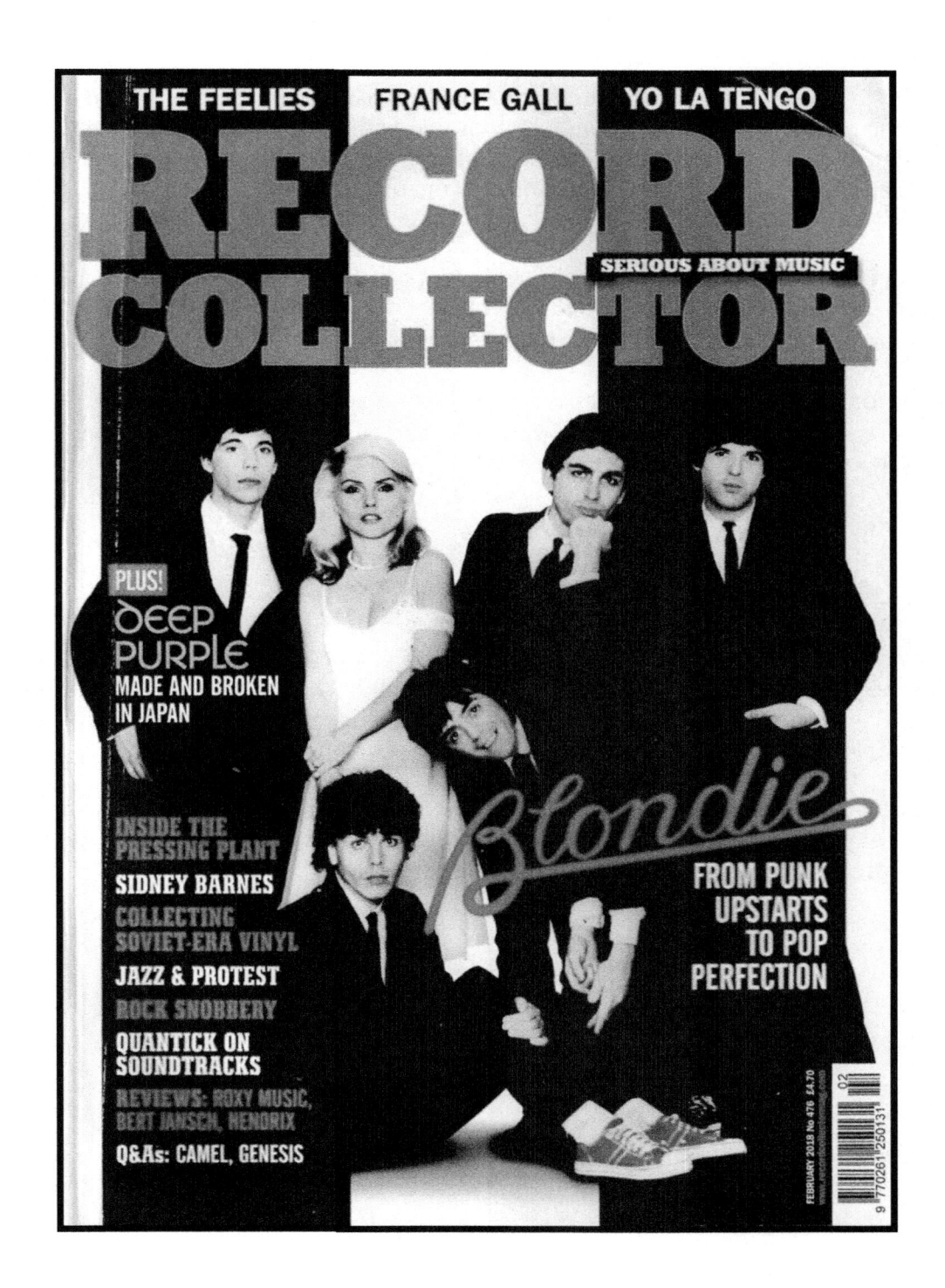

RECORD COLLECTOR

SERIOUS ABOUT MUSIC

PLUS!
DEEP PURPLE
MADE AND BROKEN IN JAPAN

INSIDE THE PRESSING PLANT
SIDNEY BARNES
COLLECTING SOVIET-ERA VINYL
JAZZ & PROTEST
ROCK SNOBBERY
QUANTICK ON SOUNDTRACKS
REVIEWS: ROXY MUSIC, BERT JANSCH, HENDRIX
Q&As: CAMEL, GENESIS

Blondie
FROM PUNK UPSTARTS TO POP PERFECTION

FEBRUARY 2018 No 476 £4.70

ACKNOWLEDGEMENTS

I would like to thank Chris Cadman, my former writing partner, for helping to make my writing dreams come true. It's incredible to think how far we both have come, since we got together to compile 'The Complete Michael Jackson Discography 1972-1990', for Adrian Grant's *Off the Wall* fan magazine in 1990. Good luck with your ongoing projects, Chris ~ I will look forward to reading them in due course!

I would like to thank the online music community, who so readily share and exchange information at: ukmix (ukmix.org/forums), Haven (fatherandy2.proboards.com) & Buzzjack (buzzjack.com/forums). In particular, I would like to thank:

- 'BrainDamagell' & 'Wayne' for posting current Canadian charts on ukmix;
- 'flatdeejay' & 'ChartFreaky' for posting German chart action, and 'Indi' and 'vdoerken' for answering my queries regarding Germany, on ukmix;
- 'mario' for posting Japanese chart action, and 'danavon' for answering my queries regarding Japan, on ukmix;
- 'Davidalic' for posting Spanish chart action on ukmix;
- 'Shakyfan', 'CZB', 'trebor' & 'beatlened' for posting Irish charts on ukmix;
- 'grendizer' for posting Canadian certifications on ukmix;
- 'CZB' and 'janjensen' for posting Danish singles charts from 1979 onwards on ukmix;
- 'Hanboo' for posting and up-dating on request full UK & USA chart runs on ukmix. R.I.P., Hanboo ~ like everyone on ukmix, I was shocked and deeply saddened to learn of your passing.

If you can fill any of the gaps in the chart information in this book, or have chart runs from a country not already featured in the book, I would love to hear from you. You can contact me via email at: **craig.halstead2@ntlworld.com** ~ thank you!

CONTENTS

INTRODUCTION	7
ALL THE TOP 40 SINGLES	19
THE ALMOST TOP 40 SINGLES	109
BLONDIE'S TOP 20 SINGLES	111
SINGLES TRIVIA	114
ALL THE TOP 40 ALBUMS	127
THE ALMOST TOP 40 ALBUMS	199
BLONDIE'S TOP 15 ALBUMS	200
ALBUMS TRIVIA	203

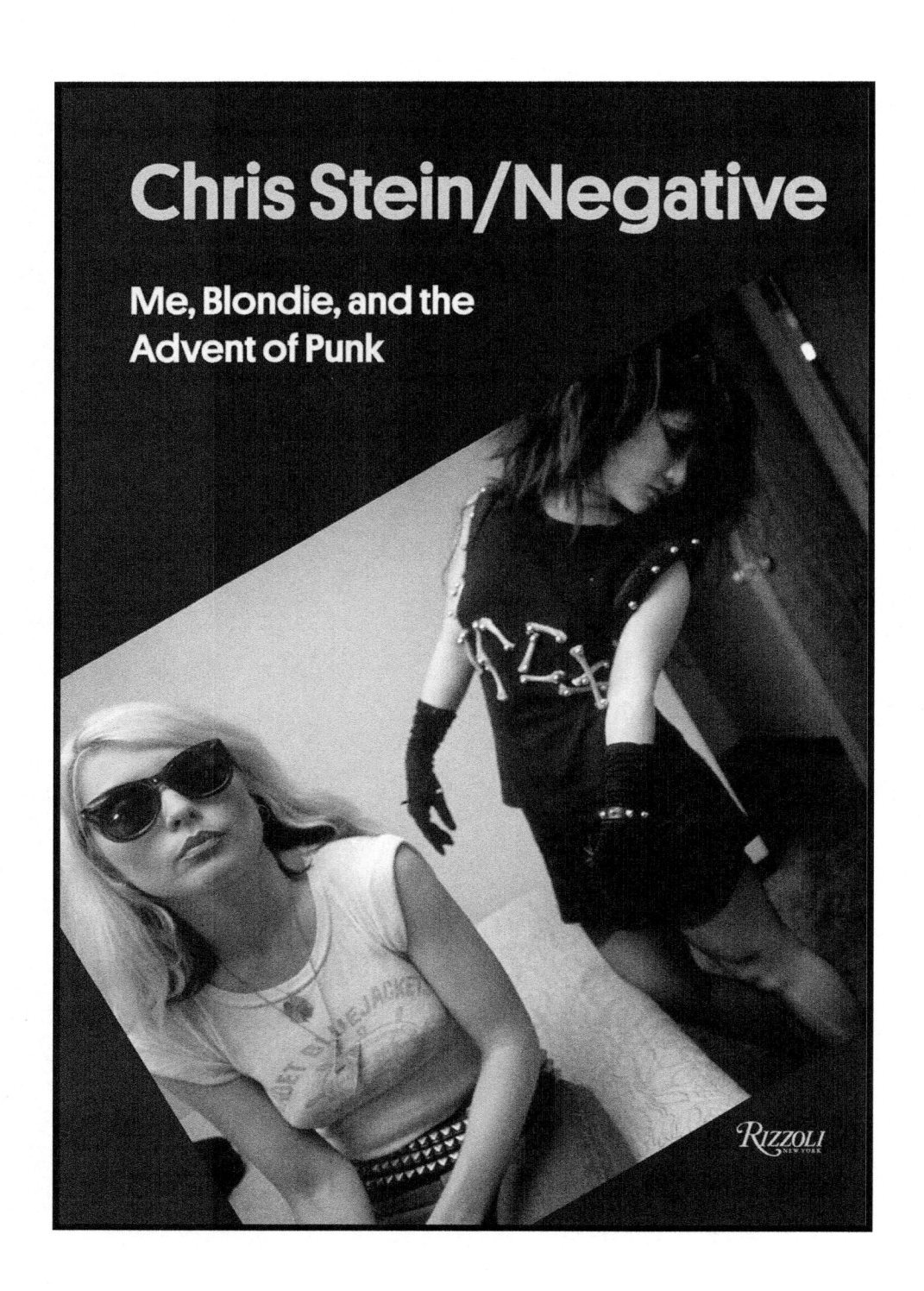

Chris Stein/Negative

Me, Blondie, and the Advent of Punk

RIZZOLI
NEW YORK

INTRODUCTION

Blondie were formed in New York by singer Debbie Harry and her guitarist boyfriend Chris Stein, after they left a band called the Stilettoes in July 1974. Originally, they were joined by ex-Stilettoes bandmates Billy O'Connor and Fred Smith, and in August 1974 the quartet performed two gigs as Angel & The Snakes. A couple of months later, inspired by 'Hey, Blondie!' catcalls directed at Debbie, the band renamed themselves Blondie.

By mid-1975, Cooper and Smith had left the band, and were replaced by Clem Burke (drums), Gary Valentine (bass guitar) and Jimmy Destri (keyboards).

Debbie Harry

Angela Trimble was born on 1st July 1945 in Miami, Florida. She was just three months old when she was adopted by Richard & Catherine Harry, and renamed Deborah Ann Harry.

Debbie learned of her adoption when she was four, but it wasn't until the late 1980s that she traced her birth mother, a concert pianist. 'The detective tried to ask her a few things,' said Debbie, 'but I think her exact words were, "Please do not bother me ever again. I do not want to be disturbed".' Debbie respected her birth mother's decision and didn't push to establish contact with her.

Debbie began her musical career in the late 1960s, when she joined the folk rock group The Wind in the Willows as a backing singer. The group's debut, self-titled album, was released in 1968, as was a single, *Moments Spent*. As well as vocals, Debbie was credited with playing tamboura, tambourine and finger cymbals on the album, which like *Moments Spent* wasn't a hit anywhere.

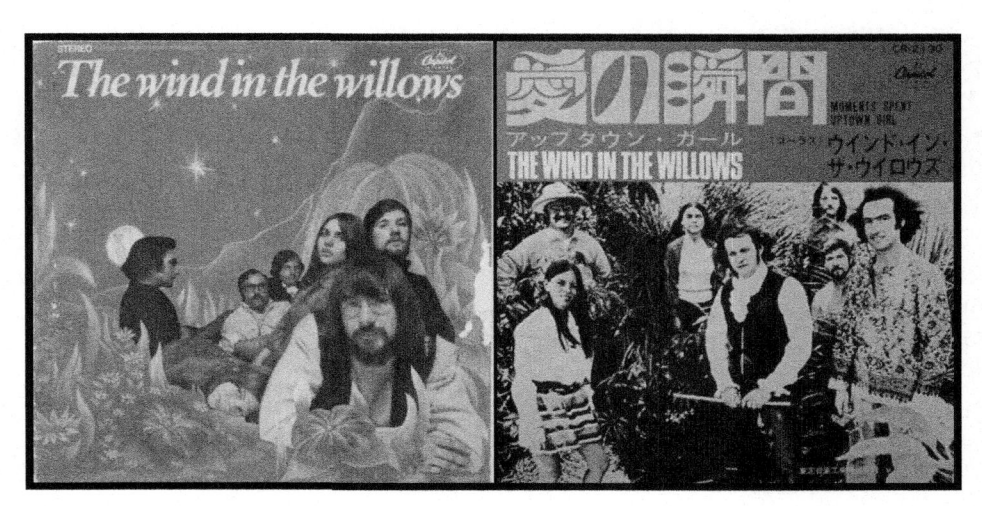

In early 1974, with Amanda Jones and Elda Gentile, Debbie formed the Stilettoes. It wasn't long before guitarist Chris Stein joined the group, and he and Debbie became a couple.

However, their time with the Stilettoes was brief, and they left the band in July 1974, and formed their own band, Angel & The Snake, which after playing a couple of gigs was renamed Blondie.

Outside Blondie, Debbie ~ or Deborah as she now prefers to be credited ~ has released five solo albums, most recently *NECESSARY EVIL* in 2007.

Chris Stein

Christopher Stein was born on 5th January 1950 in Brooklyn, New York.

Chris and Debbie first met when, briefly, he joined the Stilettoes in 1974. As well as a guitarist and songwriter, Chris is also an accomplished photographer, and his book *Negative: Me, Blondie, And The Advent Of Punk* was published in 2014.

In 1983, Chris was diagnosed with pemphigus vulgaris, a rare autoimmune disease that affects the skin. For a time, Debbie put her career on hold, to take care of him. Chris and Debbie never married and, although they broke up as a couple in 1989, they remained friends and continued to work together.

Chris did marry in 1999, and he and his wife, actress Barbara Sicuranza, have two daughters, Akira and Valentina.

Clem Burke

Clement Anthony Bozewski was born on 24th November 1954 in Bayonne, New Jersey.

In the late 1960s and early 1970s, Clem was the drummer with Total Environment and the Sweet Willie Jam Band, who were both covers bands. He also played with the Saint Andrew Bridgmen Drum & Bugle Corps, before he was recruited by Debbie and Chris, joining Blondie in 1975.

When Fred Smith quit the fledgling band, to join Television, Debbie and Chris considered disbanding Blondie. Clem was instrumental in keeping the band together, and recruited his friend and bassist Gary Valentine, to replace Smith.

Blondie did disband in 1982, following the release of the band's sixth studio album, *THE HUNTER*, and didn't reform until 1997. In the intervening years, Clem played drums with numerous other artists including the Romantics, Bob Dylan, Dramarama, Eurythmics, Iggy Pop, Joan Jett, Pete Townsend and The Ramones.

In December 2011, Clem formed The International Swingers with singer Gary Twinn (Supernaut), Glen Matlock (Sex Pistols) and James Stevenson (Generation X). The quartet's debut, self-titled album was released in 2015.

Gary Valentine

Gary Joseph Lachman was born on 24th December 1955 in Bayonne, New Jersey.

After Fred Smith quit Blondie in 1975, Gary was recruited to replace him by his friend, Clem. He wrote Blondie's debut single, *X Offender*, but left the band in 1977, and was replaced by Nigel Harrison.

Gary released a solo single, *The First One* b/w *Tomorrow Belongs To You*, in 1978 but it wasn't a hit. In February 1979, with Joel Turrisi and Richard d'Andrea, he formed the trio The Know. A single, *I Like Girls*, followed in early 1980, but the failure to secure an album deal led to the trio's break-up.

When Blondie reformed in 1997, Gary was invited to rejoin the band, and played several major festival concerts with Blondie in the United States. Ultimately, however, he was excluded from recording a new album with Blondie and taking part in the band's reunion tour.

Jimmy Destri

James Mollica Destri was born on 13th April 1954 in Brooklyn, New York.

Jimmy formed his first band, 86 Proof, while still in high school. In the early 1970s, he played in a band called Milk'N'Cookies, before joining Blondie in 1975. Along with Debbie and Chris, he emerged as one of the band's principal songwriters, and was responsible for hits such as *Picture This*, *Atomic* and the band's comeback single, *Maria*.

With Blondie taking a break from recording and touring in late 1980/early 1981, Jimmy took the opportunity to record what proved to be his only solo album, *HEART ON A WALL*, released in 1981.

Jimmy rejoined Blondie when the band reformed in 1997, and recorded 1999's *NO EXIT* and 2003's *THE CURSE OF BLONDIE* with the band. The following year, he retired from touring, but he did plan to carry on recording with Blondie. However, there was an eight year gap to the band's next studio album, 2011's *PANIC OF GIRLS*, and Jimmy wasn't involved in either the writing for or the recording of the album.

Nigel Harrison

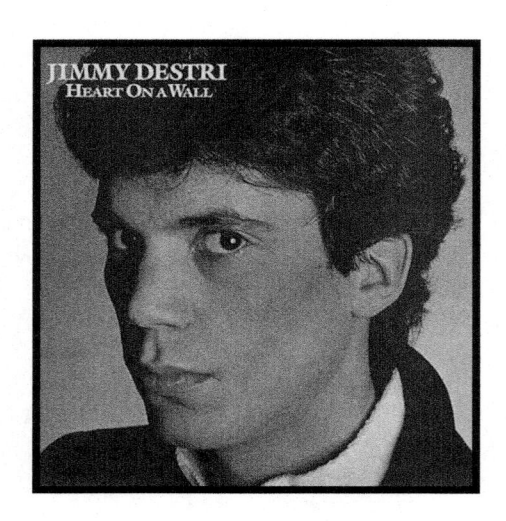

Nigel Harrison was born on 24th April 1951 in Stockport, England.

Nigel was the bassist with a local band, Farm, before going on to record and tour with Silverhead between 1972 and 1974.

Nigel was with Nite City, a band formed by the former Doors keyboardist Ray Manzarek, when he agreed to join Blondie, to replace Gary Valentine. As well as playing bass, Nigel also contributed to the band as a songwriter, and co-wrote with Debbie hits like *One Way Or Another*, *Union City Blue* and *War Child*.

Between 1982 and 1984, along with Clem Burke, Nigel was a member of Chequered Past, a band that also included Michael Des Barres (Silverhead), Steve Jones and Tony Sales. Chequered Past released their debut, self-titled album in 1984 but it wasn't a hit.

When Blondie reformed in 1997, Nigel was originally invited to rejoin the band, and he recorded several demos for what became the *NO EXIT* album. However, he was excluded from the band before the album was completed, which led to a major dispute and an unsuccessful lawsuit.

More recently, Nigel has played with a band called The Grabs, who have released two albums, *SEX, FASHION & MONEY* in 2005 and *POLITICAL DISCO* in 2010.

Blondie signed with Private Stock Records, and released their debut album *BLONDIE* in December 1976, but initially at least it wasn't successful. The following September, the band bought out their contract with Private Stock Records, and signed instead with a British label, Chrysalis Records, who reissued *BLONDIE*.

Blondie's debut single, *X Offender*, wasn't a hit, but thanks to a fortuitous mistake the B-side *In The Flesh* was: on the Australian TV music show *Countdown*, *In The Flesh* was mistakenly played, instead of *X Offender*. The audience reaction was very positive, and *In The Flesh* rose to no.2 on the Australian singles chart, and in the process helped *BLONDIE* to no.14 on the albums chart.

Blondie's second album, *PLASTIC LETTERS*, was moderately successful, but it really wasn't until the band's third album *PARALLEL LINES* was released that global success on a massive scale really took off.

Like many bands, Blondie's line-up has changed several times over the years. The band is still active today, and this is Blondie's current line-up:

- Debbie Harry
- Chris Stein
- Clem Burke
- Leigh Foxx (bass, since 2004)
- Matt Katz-Bohen (keyboards, since 2008)
- Tommy Kessler (guitar, since 2010)

Blondie was inducted into the Rock 'N' Roll Hall of Fame on 13th March 2006.

All The Top 40 Hits

For the purposes of this book, to qualify as a Top 40 hit, a single or album must have entered the Top 40 singles/albums chart in at least one of the following featured countries: Australia, Austria, Canada (singles only), Belgium (Flanders), Denmark (singles only), Finland, France, Germany, Ireland (singles only), Italy, Japan, Netherlands, New Zealand, Norway, South Africa (singles only), Spain, Sweden, Switzerland, United Kingdom, United States of America and Zimbabwe.

The Top 40 singles and albums are detailed chronologically, according to the date they first entered the chart in one or more of the featured countries. Each Top 40 single and album is illustrated and the catalogue numbers and release dates are detailed, for both Australia and the UK, followed by the chart runs in each featured country, including any chart re-entries. Where full chart runs are unavailable, peak position and weeks on the chart are given.

For both singles and albums, the main listing is followed by 'The Almost Top 40 Singles/Albums', which gives an honorable mention to singles/albums that peaked between no.41 and no.50 in one or more countries. There is also a points-based list of Blondie & Deborah Harry's most successful singles and albums, plus a fascinating 'Trivia' section at the end of each section which looks at the most successful singles and albums in each of the featured countries.

The Charts

The charts from an increasing number of countries are now freely available online, and for many countries it is possible to research weekly chart runs. Although this book focuses on Top 40 hits, longer charts runs are included where available, up to the Top 100 for countries where a Top 100 or longer is published. Where full chart runs are unavailable, peak positions and weeks on the chart are detailed.

Nowadays, charts are compiled and published on a weekly basis – in the past, however, some countries published charts on a bi-weekly or monthly basis, and most charts listed far fewer titles than they do today. There follows a summary of the current charts from each country featured in this book, together with relevant online resources and chart books.

Australia
Current charts: Top 100 Singles & Top 100 Albums.
Online resources: current weekly Top 50 Singles & Albums, but no archive, at **ariacharts.com.au**; archive of complete weekly charts dating back to 2001 at **pandora.nla.gov.au/tep/23790**; searchable archive of Top 50 Singles & Albums dating back to 1988 at **australian-charts.com**.
Books: 'Australian Chart Book 1970-1992' & 'Australian Chart Book 1993-2009' by David Kent.

Austria
Current charts: Top 75 Singles & Top 75 Albums.
Online resources: current weekly charts and a searchable archive dating back to 1965 for singles and 1973 for albums at **austriancharts.at**.

Belgium
Current charts: Top 50 Singles & Top 200 Albums for two different regions, Flanders (the Dutch speaking north of the country) and Wallonia (the French speaking south).
Online resources: current weekly charts and a searchable archive dating back to 1995 for albums, and pre-1976 for singles, at **ultratop.be**.
Book: '*Het Belgisch Hitboek – 40 Jaar Hits In Vlaanderen*' by Robert Collin.
Note: the information in this book for Belgium relates to the Flanders region.

Canada
Current charts: Hot 100 Singles & Top 100 Albums.
Online resources: weekly charts and a searchable archive of weekly charts from the Nielsen SoundScan era at **billboard.com/biz** (subscription only); weekly charts are posted on **ukmix.org**.
Book: 'The Canadian Singles Chart Book 1975-1996' by Nanda Lwin.
Note: the information in this book is taken from Nanda Lwin's book, so relates to singles from 1975-1996 only.

Denmark
Current Charts: Top 40 Singles & Albums.
Online resources: weekly charts and a fully searchable archive at **danishcharts.com**, however, this only goes back to 2001. In 2001, the chart was a weekly Top 20, which expanded to a Top 40 in November 2007. No archive currently exists for charts before 2001. 'CZB' has posted

weekly Top 20s from September 1994 to December 1999 on **ukmix.org**, and 'janjensen' has posted the Top 10/15 singles from January 1979 onwards on the same forum. This means no album charts before September 1994 are available, and there is no information for 2000.

Finland
Current charts: Top 20 Singles & Top 50 Albums.
Online resources: current weekly charts and a searchable archive dating back to 1995 at **finnishcharts.com**.
Book: *Sisältää Hitin* by Timo Pennanem.

France
Current charts: Top 200 Singles Albums.
Online resources: current weekly charts and a searchable archive dating back to 1984 for singles and 1997 for albums at **lescharts.com**; searchable archive for earlier/other charts at **infodisc.fr**.
Book: '*Hit Parades 1950-1998*' by Daniel Lesueur.
Note: Compilation albums were excluded from the main chart until 2008, when a Top 200 Comprehensive chart was launched.

Germany
Current charts: Top 100 Singles & Top 100 Albums.
Online resources: current weekly charts (Top 10s only) and a searchable archive dating back to 2007 (again, Top 10s only) at **germancharts.com**; complete Top 100 charts are usually posted weekly in the German Charts Thread on **ukmix.org**.
Books: '*Deutsche Chart Singles 1956-1980*', '*Deutsche Chart Singles 1981-90*', '*Deutsche Chart Singles 1991-1995*' & '*Deutsche Chart LP's 1962-1986*' published by Taurus Press.

Ireland
Current charts: Top 100 Singles & Top 100 Albums.
Online resources: current weekly charts are published at IRMA (**irma.ie**); there is a searchable archive for Top 30 singles (entry date, peak position and week on chart only) at **irishcharts.ie**; an annual Irish Chart Thread has been published annually from 2007 to date, plus singles charts from 1967 to 1999 and album charts for 1993, 1995-6 and 1999, have been published at ukmix (**ukmix.org**); weekly album charts from March 2003 to date can be found at **acharts.us/ireland_albums_top_75**.
Note: the information presented in this book is for singles only.

Italy
Current charts: Top 100 Singles & Top 100 Albums.
Online resources: weekly charts and a weekly chart archive dating back to 2005 at **fimi.it**; a searchable archive of Top 20 charts dating back to 2000 at **italiancharts.com**; pre-2000 information has been posted at ukmix (**ukmix.org**).
Books: *Musica e Dischi Borsa Singoli 1960-2019* & *Musica e Dischi Borsa Album 1964-2019* by Guido Racca.

Note: as the FIMI-Neilsen charts didn't start until 1995, the information detailed in this book is from the Musica & Dischi chart.

Japan
Current charts: Top 200 Singles & Top 300 Albums.
Online resources: current weekly charts (in Japanese) at **oricon.co.jp/rank**; selected information is available on the Japanese Chart/The Newest Charts and Japanese Chart/The Archives threads at **ukmix.org**.

Netherlands
Current charts: Top 100 Singles & Top 100 Albums.
Online resources: current weekly charts and a searchable archive dating back to 1956 for singles and 1969 for albums at **dutchcharts.nl**.

New Zealand
Current charts: Top 40 Singles & Top 40 Albums.
Online resources: current weekly charts and a searchable archive dating back to 1975 at **charts.org.nz**.
Book: 'The Complete New Zealand Music Charts 1966-2006' by Dean Scapolo.

Norway
Current charts: Top 20 Singles & Top 40 Albums.
Online resources: current weekly charts and a searchable archive dating back to 1958 for singles and 1967 for albums at **norwegiancharts.com**.

South Africa
Current charts: no official charts.
Online resources: none known.
Book: 'South Africa Chart Book' by Christopher Kimberley.
Notes: the singles chart was discontinued in early 1989, as singles were no longer being manufactured in significant numbers. The albums chart only commenced in December 1981, and was discontinued in 1995, following re-structuring of the South African Broadcasting Corporation.

Spain
Current charts: Top 50 Singles & Top 100 Albums.
Online resources: current weekly charts and a searchable archive dating back to 2005 at **spanishcharts.com**.
Book: *'Sólo éxitos 1959-2002 Año a Año'* by Fernando Salaverri.

Sweden
Current charts: Top 60 Singles & Top 100 Albums.
Online resources: current weekly charts and a searchable archive dating back to 1975 at **swedishcharts.com**.

Switzerland
Current charts: Top 75 Singles & Top 100 Albums.
Online resources: current weekly charts and a searchable archive dating back to 1968 for singles and 1983 for albums at **hitparade.ch**.

UK
Current Charts: Top 100 Singles & Top 200 Albums.
Online resources: current weekly Top 100 charts and a searchable archive dating back to 1960 at **officialcharts.com**; weekly charts are posted on a number of music forums, including ukmix (**ukmix.org**), Haven (**fatherandy2.proboards.com**) and Buzzjack (**buzzjack.com**).
Note: Weekly Top 200 albums charts are only available via subscription from UK ChartsPlus (**ukchartsplus.co.uk**).

USA
Current charts: Hot 100 Singles & Billboard 200 Albums.
Online resources: current weekly charts are available at **billboard.com**, however, to access Billboard's searchable archive at **billboard.com/biz** you must be a subscriber; weekly charts are posted on a number of music forums, including ukmix (**ukmix.org**), Haven (**fatherandy2.proboards.com**) and Buzzjack (**buzzjack.com**).
Note: older 'catalog' albums (i.e. albums older than two years) were excluded from the Billboard 200 before December 2009, so the chart didn't accurately reflect the country's best-selling albums. Therefore, in this book Billboard's Top Comprehensive Albums chart has been used from December 2003 to December 2009, as this did include all albums. In December 2009 the Top Comprehensive Albums chart became the Billboard 200, and Billboard launched a new Top Current Albums chart – effectively, the old Billboard 200.

Zimbabwe
Current charts: no official charts.
Online resources: none known.
Books: 'Zimbabwe Singles Chart Book' by Christopher Kimberley.
Note: Zimbabwe was, of course, known as Rhodesia before 1980, but the country is referred to by its present name throughout this book.

All The Top 40 Singles

ROXODUS

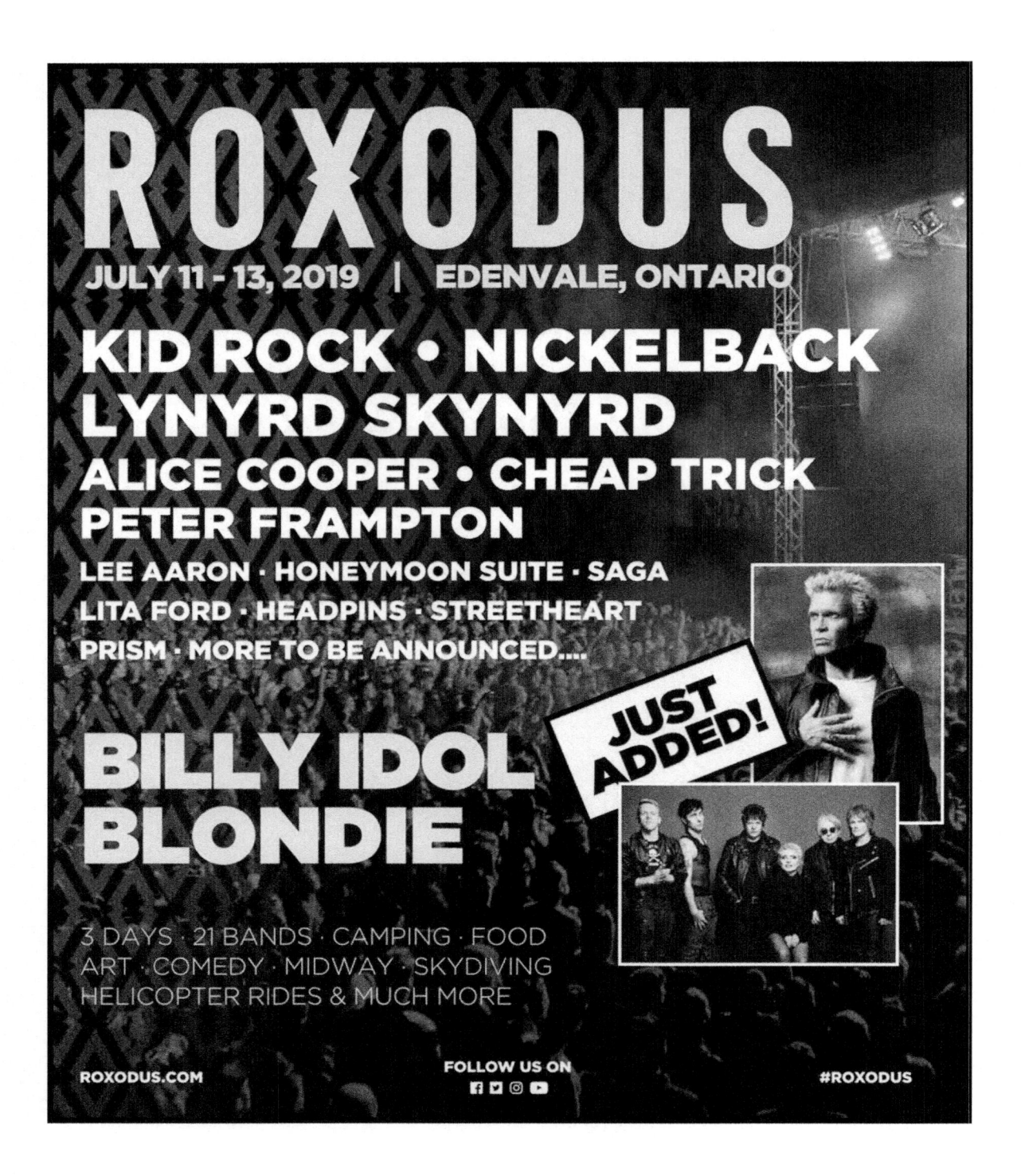

JULY 11 - 13, 2019 | EDENVALE, ONTARIO

KID ROCK • NICKELBACK
LYNYRD SKYNYRD
ALICE COOPER • CHEAP TRICK
PETER FRAMPTON

LEE AARON • HONEYMOON SUITE • SAGA
LITA FORD • HEADPINS • STREETHEART
PRISM • MORE TO BE ANNOUNCED....

BILLY IDOL
BLONDIE

JUST ADDED!

3 DAYS • 21 BANDS • CAMPING • FOOD
ART • COMEDY • MIDWAY • SKYDIVING
HELICOPTER RIDES & MUCH MORE

ROXODUS.COM   FOLLOW US ON   #ROXODUS

1 ~ IN THE FLESH

USA: Not released.

UK: Chrysalis CHS 2180 (1977).
  A-side: *Rip Her To Shreds*.
  B-side: *In The Flesh/X Offender*.

In The Flesh was released as the B-side to *Rip Her To Shreds* in the UK, but neither was a hit.

Australia
5.09.77: peaked at no.**2**, charted for 24 weeks

Belgium
30.01.82: **40**

Blondie's debut single, *X Offender*, was written by Debbie Harry and Gary Valentine for the group's self-titled debut album, which was released in 1976.
  X Offender wasn't a hit, and neither initially was the follow-up *In The Flesh*, composed by Debbie and Chris Stein. Then, on the Australia TV show *Countdown*, *In The Flesh* was mistakenly played instead of *X Offender*, and was very well received by the show's audience. This led to the single being re-released, and it gave Blondie their first hit anywhere, rising to no.2 on the Australian singles chart.

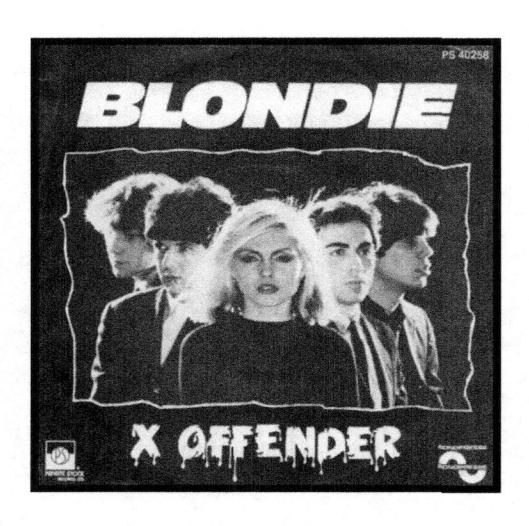

In the UK, Europe and Japan, *In The Flesh* and *X Offender* were released on the B-side of *Rip Her To Shreds*, which failed to chart in most countries, but was a minor no.81 hit in Australia.

2 ~ DENIS

USA: Chrysalis CHS 2200 (1978).
   B-side: *I'm On E*.

Denis wasn't a hit in the United States.

UK: Chrysalis CHS 2204 (1977).
   B-side: *Contact In Red Square/Kung Fu Girls*.

18.02.78: 50-33-11-5-**2-2-2-2**-5-10-20-34-47-71
3.12.88: 62-50-58 (remix)

Australia
17.04.78: peaked at no.**12**, charted for 17 weeks

Austria
15.05.78: 12-**10**-24-22 (monthly)

Belgium
4.03.78: 20-9-3-2-**1-1-1-1**-5-11-22

France
14.04.78: peaked at no.**50**, charted for 12 weeks

Germany
24.04.78: 17-18-12-13-**9**-13-14-14-14-27-29-34-35-44-40

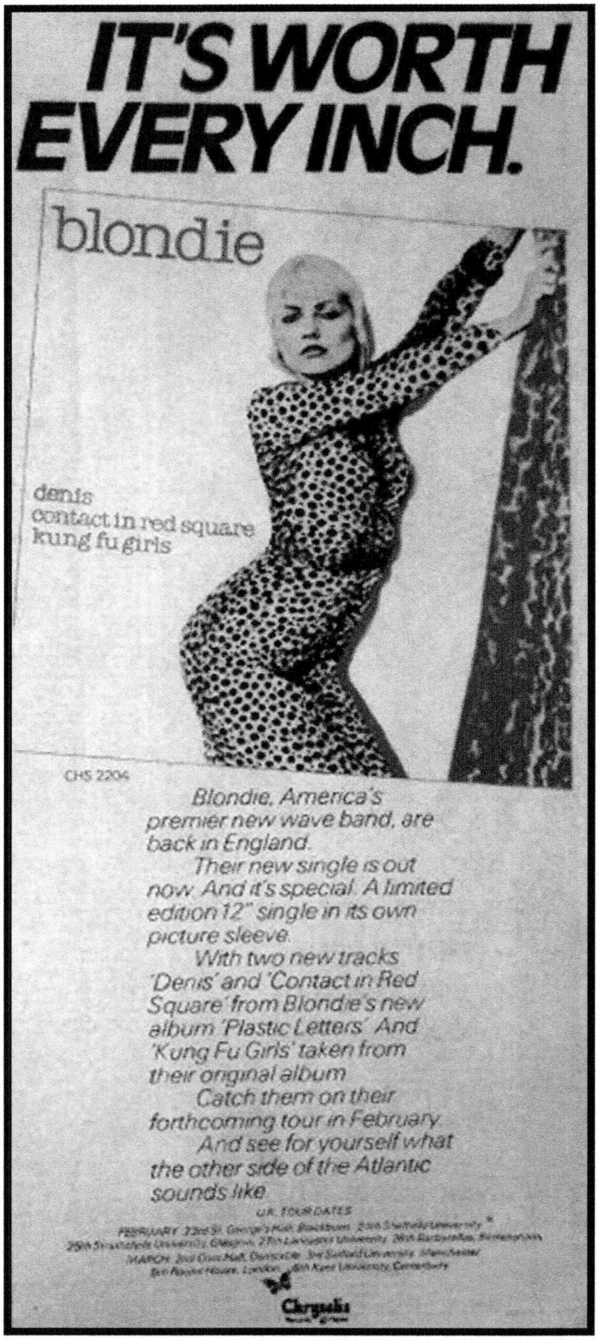
IT'S WORTH EVERY INCH.
blondie
denis
contact in red square
kung fu girls
CHS 2204
Blondie, America's premier new wave band, are back in England.
Their new single is out now. And it's special. A limited edition 12" single in its own picture sleeve.
With two new tracks 'Denis' and 'Contact in Red Square' from Blondie's new album 'Plastic Letters'. And 'Kung Fu Girls' taken from their original album.
Catch them on their forthcoming tour in February.
And see for yourself what the other side of the Atlantic sounds like.
U.K. TOUR DATES
Chrysalis

Ireland
23.03.78: 13-**3-3-3**-4-5-10-12-17

Netherlands
25.02.78: 14-2-**1-1-1-1-1-1**-7-7-13-21

New Zealand
26.02.89: 50-x-**30**-44-50 (remix)

Sweden
25.08.78: **19** (bi-weekly)

Zimbabwe
22.07.78: peaked at no.**11**, charted for 7 weeks

Denise, as the song was originally titled, was written by Neil Levenson, inspired by his childhood friend, Denise Lefrak. Randy & The Rainbows recorded the song in 1963, and as a single *Denise* rose to no.10 on the Hot 100 in the United States, and was a no.5 hit in Canada.

Blondie re-titled *Denise* to the masculine *Denis* (pronounced 'Denee'), and covered the song for their second album, *PLASTIC LETTERS*, released in 1978.

As the lead single from the album, *Denis* gave Blondie their first international hit. The single spent six weeks at no.1 in the Netherlands, and rose to no.2 in the UK, denied the top spot first by Kate Bush's *Wuthering Heights*, and then by Brian & Michael's *Matchstalk Men And Matchstalk Cats And Dogs*. Elsewhere, *Denis* charted at no.1 in Belgium, no.3 in Ireland, no.9 in Germany, no.10 in Austria, no.11 in Zimbabwe, no.12 in Australia, no.19 in Sweden and no.50 in France.

In 1988, a remixed version of *Denis* featured on Blondie & Debbie Harry's remix compilation, *ONCE MORE INTO THE BLEACH*. Issued as a single, the remixed version achieved no.30 in New Zealand and no.50 in the UK.

In 2002, the Dutch actress and singer Georgina Verbaan recorded a cover of *Denis* for her debut album, *SUGAR SPIDER*. Released as a single, her version of *Denis* achieved no.30 in the Netherlands.

3 ~ (I'M ALWAYS TOUCHED BY YOUR) PRESENCE DEAR

USA: not released.

UK: Chrysalis CHS 2217 (1978).
  B-side: *Poets Problem/Detroit 442*.

6.05.78: 35-19-20-**10**-15-17-34-54-71

Belgium
13.05.78: 27-17-17-17-15-15-**14**-18

Netherlands
27.05.78: 13-**8**-**8**-13-10-22-40-40

(I'm Always Touched By Your) Presence Dear was written by Blondie's bass guitarist, Gary Valentine, for his girlfriend at the time, journalist Lisa Jane Persky.
   'During the Iggy (Pop) tour, we discovered we were having the same kind of dreams or found we were thinking of each other at the same time,' Valentine explained. 'Although we were thousands of miles apart, we were still in touch. Thinking of this one afternoon, it all came together in a song.'
   Blondie recorded *(I'm Always Touched By Your) Presence Dear* for their *PLASTIC LETTERS* album, and it was released as the follow-up to *Denis* in most countries, excluding the United States. However, it failed to repeat the success *Denis* enjoyed, only charting at no.8 in the Netherlands, no.10 in the UK and no.14 in Belgium.

I'M ALWAYS TOUCHED BY YOUR PRESENCE DEAR.......
LISTEN...
TO THE NEW, LIMITED EDITION, TWELVE INCH SINGLE FROM BLONDIE I'M ALWAYS TOUCHED BY YOUR PRESENCE DEAR (SOB) POETS PROBLEM AND DETROIT 442
LATER...
THE ALBUMS...
BLONDIE (GULP) PLASTIC LETTERS
Chrysalis

Tracey Ullman recorded a cover of *(I'm Always Touched By Your) Presence Dear* for her debut album, *YOU BROKE MY HEART IN 17 PLACES*, released in 1983. Twelve years later, Annie Lennox recorded a version of the song, which featured on some formats of her 1995 single, *A Whiter Shade Of Pale*.

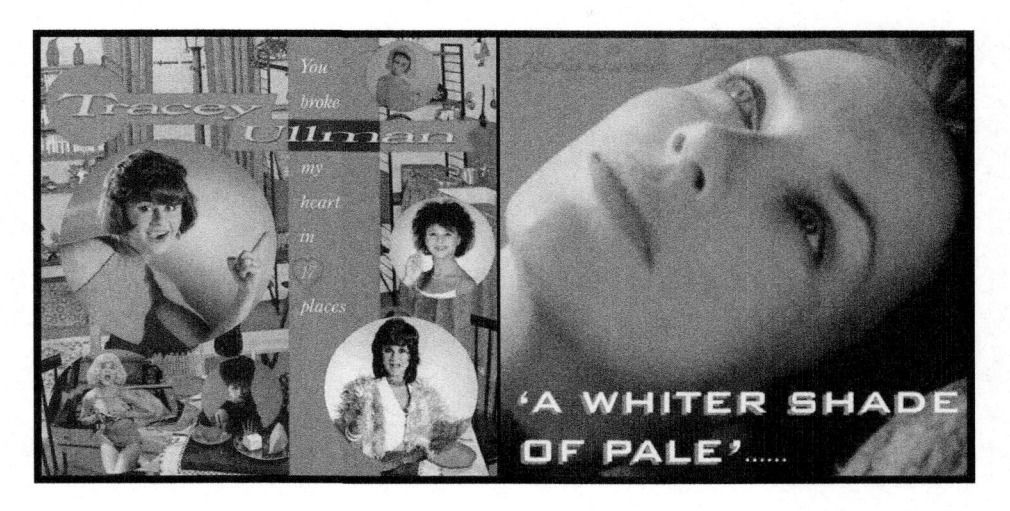

Gary Valentine recorded his own version of *(I'm Always Touched By Your) Presence Dear* for his 2003 compilation, *TOMORROW BELONGS TO YOU*.

(I'm Always Touched By Your) Presence Dear

Words and Music by GARY VALENTINE

Recorded on CHRYSALIS by **BLONDIE**

EMI Music Publishing Ltd • 138/140 Charing Cross Road • London WC2H 0LD

4 ~ PICTURE THIS

USA: not released.

UK: Chrysalis CHS 2242 (1978).
  B-side: *Fade Away (And Radiate)*.

26.08.78: 61-23-16-13-**12-12**-14-18-24-44-66

Australia
18.06.79: peaked at no.**88**, charted for 4 weeks

Ireland
15.09.78: 26-17-**13**-30

Sweden
6.10.78: **15** (bi-weekly)

Picture This was composed by Debbie Harry (lyrics) with Chris Stein & Jimmy Destri (music), and recorded by Blondie for their third album, *PARALLEL LINES*, released in late 1978.
  Outside the United States, *Picture This* was issued as the album's lead single. It charted at no.12 in the UK, no.13 in Ireland and no.15 in Sweden, but was only a minor no.88 hit in Australia.

Blondie
Picture This
THE NEW SINGLE
Limited Edition
Blonde Vinyl
And Picture Bag
CHS 2242
Watch Out For Blondie's New
Album 'Parallel Lines' CDL 1192.
Chrysalis

5 ~ I'M GONNA LOVE YOU TOO

USA: Chrysalis CHS 2251 (1978).
  B-side: *Just Go Away*.

I'm Gonna Love You Too wasn't a hit in the United States.

UK: not released.

Belgium
9.09.78: 28-17-12-6-6-5-**3**-6-15-25

Netherlands
9.09.78: 21-8-8-7-7-**6**-**6**-14-32-36

I'm Gonna Love You Too is generally credited to Joe B. Mauldin, Norman Petty and Niki Sullivan, however, some observers believe the primary writer was actually Buddy Holly, with Jerry Allison composing the bridge.
    There is no question Buddy Holly originally recorded *I'm Gonna Love You Too*, which he did in 1957 for his second, self-titled album. Holly's version was released as a single, but it wasn't a hit.

Blondie recorded *I'm Gonna Love You Too* for their 1978 album, *PARALLEL LINES*, and it was released as the lead single in the United States and Netherlands. It wasn't a hit in the United States, but the single achieved no.3 in Belgium and spent two weeks at no.6 in the Netherlands.

Numerous artists have recorded covers of *I'm Gonna Love You Too* over the years, including Adam Faith, Terry Jacks and Denny Laine of Wings and Moody Blues fame.

6 ~ HANGING ON THE TELEPHONE

USA: Chrysalis CHS 2271 (1978).
  B-side: *Will Anything Happen?*

Hanging On The Telephone wasn't a hit in the United States.

UK: Chrysalis CHS 2266 (1978).
  B-side: *Will Anything Happen?*

11.11.78: 27-18-9-**5**-7-10-17-17-22-43-60-71

Australia
16.07.79: peaked at no.**39**, charted for 15 weeks

Belgium
9.06.79: 24-**19**-24

Ireland
24.11.78: 29-20-**16**-20-19-27-27-29-25

Netherlands
9.06.79: 27-22-**20**-27-27-39

New Zealand
23.09.79: 50-**43**

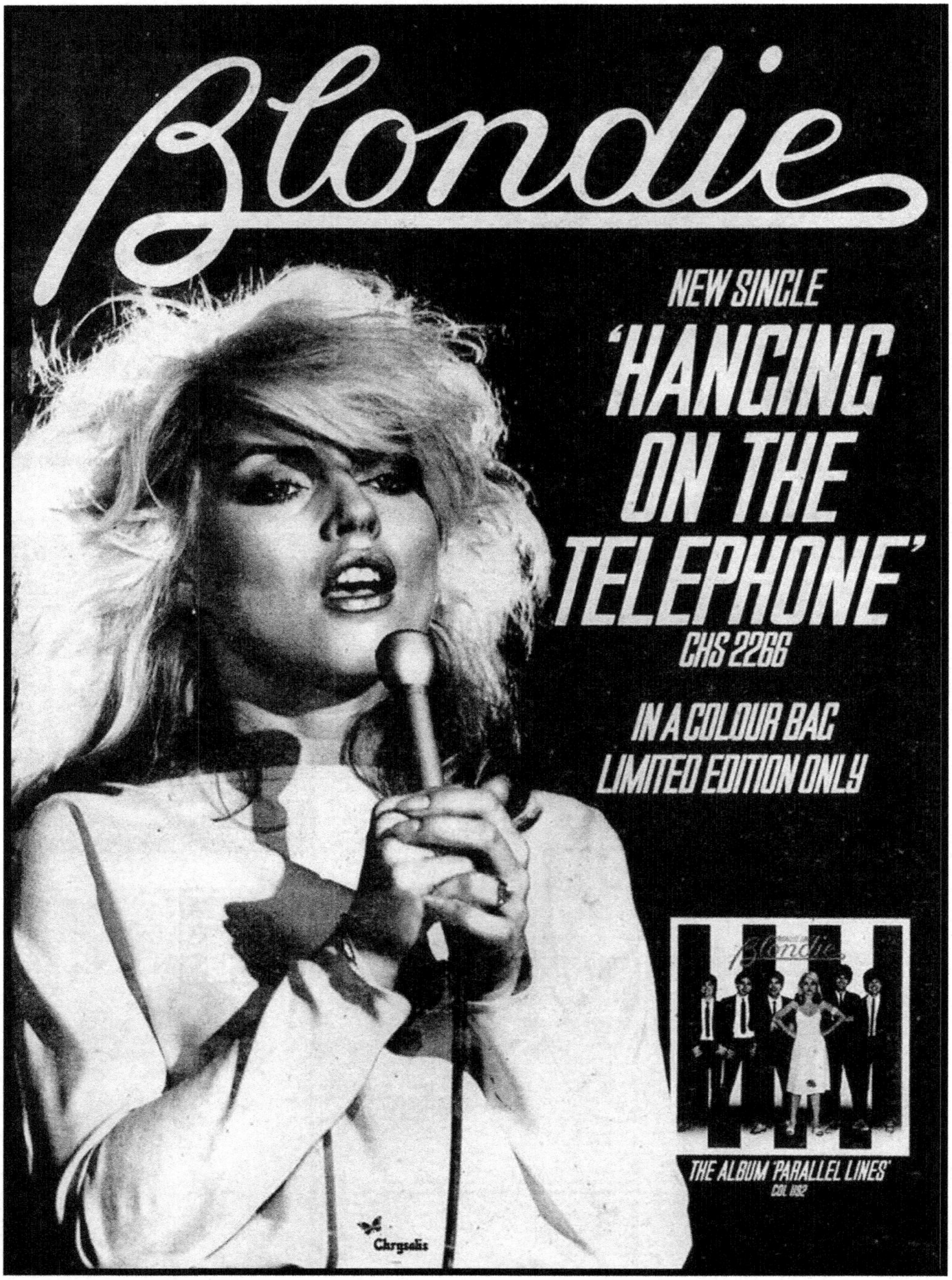
Blondie
NEW SINGLE
'HANGING ON THE TELEPHONE'
CHS 2266
IN A COLOUR BAG
LIMITED EDITION ONLY
THE ALBUM 'PARALLEL LINES'
Chrysalis

Hanging On The Telephone was composed by Jack Lee, who originally performed and recorded the song with his short-lived band The Nerves in 1976 ~ it was the lead track from the band's debut EP.

Blondie recorded a cover of *Hanging On The Telephone* for their *PARALLEL LINES* album, and it was released as the second single in most countries. The single failed to enter the Hot 100 in the United States, but it charted at no.5 in the UK, no.16 in Ireland, no.20 in the Netherlands, no.39 in Australia and no.43 in New Zealand.

7 ~ SUNDAY GIRL

USA: not released.

UK: Chrysalis CHS 2320 (1979).
  B-side: *I Know But I Don't Know*.

19.05.79: 10-**1**-**1**-**1**-2-4-7-11-31-35-68-72-74

Australia
5.03.79: peaked at no.**1** (5), charted for 24 weeks (b/w *Heart Of Glass*)

Austria
15.07.79: 9-**5**-7 (monthly)

Belgium
2.12.78: 24-**23**-27-27

Denmark
22.06.79: 10-5-**3**-**3**-7-9-7-9-10

Finland
06.79: **13** (monthly)

France
8.06.79: peaked at no.**40**, charted for 19 weeks

Blondie
NEW SINGLE
Sunday Girl
c/w Sunday Girl (French Version)
I Know But I Don't Know*
LIMITED EDITION 12" IN A PICTURE SLEEVE CHS 12 2320

Germany
18.06.79: 12-11-**6**-8-7-7-8-10-9-9-8-13-22-23-28-42-41-37

Ireland
25.05.79: 8-**1-1-1-1**-2-4-10-14

Japan
5.09.79: peaked at no.**69**, charted for 10 weeks

Netherlands
25.11.78: 22-**13**-14-18-21-39

New Zealand
16.09.79: **48** (b/w *Heart Of Glass*)

Norway
30.06.79: 9-8-**5-5**-6-**5**-6-10-8-7-8-8-10

South Africa
28.02.79: peaked at no.**8**, charted for 7 weeks

Sweden
29.06.79: **18** (bi-weekly)

Switzerland
1.07.79: 15-7-**5-5-5**-6-8-10-11-12

Zimbabwe
4.08.79: peaked at no.**3**, charted for 14 weeks

Written by Chris Stein, *Sunday Girl* was released as the fourth single from *PARALLEL LINES* in most countries, but surprisingly ~ despite the success of *Heart Of Glass* ~ it wasn't released as a single in the United States, where *One Way Or Another* was preferred.

In Australasia, *Sunday Girl* was released as the lead single from *PARALLEL LINES*, but failed to chart. Later, it was re-issued, this time as a double A-side with *Heart Of Glass* ~ which is the song which attracted all the attention. Despite this, the single charted as a double A-side, and went all the way to no.1 in Australia, but stalled at no.48 in New Zealand.

Sunday Girl also hit no.1 in Ireland and the UK, and achieved no.3 in Denmark and Zimbabwe, no.5 in Austria, Norway and Switzerland, no.6 in Germany, no.8 in South Africa, no.13 in Finland and the Netherlands, no.18 in Sweden, no.23 in Belgium and no.40 in France.

Blondie recorded a French language version of *Sunday Girl*, which was released as the B-side of the single in France and the Netherlands, and featured on the 12" single in the UK.

BRAVO

Nr. 31 26. Juli 1979 DM 1,30

C 1917 C

Neue Aufklärung:
So entsteht ein Baby

Echter Foto-Krimi:
Mord aus Einsamkeit
Ergreifendes Jungen-Schicksal

2 SUPER-POSTERS:
ELVIS + BLONDIE
Mit starken Storys

NOCH 3 POSTERS:

PETER MAFFAY · OLIVIA PASCAL

Grand-Prix-Star FERRARI

8 ~ HEART OF GLASS

USA: Chrysalis CHS 2295 (1979).
  B-side: *11:59*.

17.02.79: 84-75-57-47-26-21-15-9-8-3-**1**-2-2-10-13-15-27-38-49-63-98

UK: Chrysalis CHS 2275 (1979).
  B-side: *Rifle Range*.

27.01.79: 6-**1**-**1**-**1**-**1**-2-6-8-24-38-58-73
8.07.95: 15-35-58-93 (remix)

Australia
5.03.79: peaked at no.**1** (5), charted for 24 weeks (b/w *Sunday Girl*)

Austria
15.03.79: 20-**1**-**1**-7-20 (monthly)

Belgium
3.03.79: 20-8-**5**-6-7-10-13-18-24

Canada
2.05.79: peaked at no.**1** (6), charted for 28 weeks

HEART OF GLASS
Words and Music by
DEBORAH HARRY & CHRIS STEIN
Recorded by
Blondie
on CHRYSALIS Records
EMI MUSIC
EMI Music Publishing Ltd • 138/140 Charing Cross Road • London WC2H 0LD
E

Denmark
23.03.79: 8-10-8-7
18.05.79: **4**-6-**4**-9-6-7-**4**-8-8-9-8-8-8-9

Finland
03.79: peaked at no.**11**, charted for 2 months

France
3.02.79: peaked at no.**4**, charted for 35 weeks

Germany
19.02.79: 21-2-**1-1-1-1-1-1**-2-2-3-3-3-6-4-5-9-16-13-22-22-25-32-35-37-42-43-46

Ireland
9.02.79: 6-**2-2**-3-**2**-3-3-7-16-30

Italy
10.03.79: peaked at no.**8**, charted for 19 weeks

Japan
20.04.79: peaked at no.**30**, charted for 19 weeks

Netherlands
24.02.79: 12-11-9-**8**-9-15-19-33-49

New Zealand
25.03.79: 13-7-4-2-**1**-2-**1-1-1**-2-3-3-5-10-16-20-19-23-26-26-35-37-34
16.09.79: 48 (b/w *Sunday Girl*)

Norway
3.03.79: 9-7-7-6-**5-5**-7-7

South Africa
7.04.79: peaked at no.**2**, charted for 17 weeks

Spain
4.06.79: peaked at no.**10**, charted for 16 weeks

Sweden
9.03.79: 12-5-**3**-9-8-8-9-12-14-12-14-x-x-14 (bi-weekly)

Switzerland
25.02.79: 14-9-6-3-2-**1-1-1**-2-5-7-8-11-13

Zimbabwe
28.04.79: peaked at no.1 (1), charted for 16 weeks

Heart Of Glass was written by Debbie Harry and Chris Stein, and was released as the third single from *PARALLEL LINES* ~ ahead of *Sunday Girl* ~ in most countries.

Inspired by the Hues Corporation hit *Rock The Boat*, the song was originally written in 1974-5 as *Once I Had A Love*, and a demo version was recorded in 1975. Three years later a second, poppier demo was recorded, with the same title, but again the band weren't happy with the result.

'*Heart Of Glass* was one of the first songs Blondie wrote,' said Debbie, 'but it was years before we recoded it properly. We'd tried it as a ballad, as reggae, but it never quite worked.'

It wasn't until Blondie were working with producer Mike Chapman on the album that would become *PARALLEL LINES* that the song was re-visited, re-titled *Heart Of Glass* and given a distinct disco vibe.

'When we did *Heart Of Glass* it wasn't too cool in our social set to play disco,' said Debbie, 'but we did it because we wanted to be uncool ... we spent three hours just getting the bass drum. It was the hardest song to do on the album and took us the longest in studio hours.'

In an interview with *New Musical Express* magazine in February 1978, Debbie confessed she was a fan of the Euro disco music of Giorgio Moroder, saying 'it's commercial, but it's good, it says something – that's the kind of stuff I want to do.'

Three months later, at the Johnny Blitz Benefit concert, Blondie surprised everyone by including Donna Summer's *I Feel Love* in their set-list.

Heart Of Glass proved controversial for two reasons.

One, Blondie were accused of 'selling out' by some of their fans, who were dismayed the band had recorded a disco track. And two, the song included the lyric 'pain in the ass'.

'We weren't thinking about selling out,' said Chris Stein, 'we were thinking about Kraftwerk and Euro-electric music ... it brought black and white music together.'

'At first,' said Debbie, 'the song kept saying "Once I had love, it was a gas. Soon turned out, it was a pain in the ass". We couldn't keep saying that, so we came up with "Soon turned out, had a heart of glass". We kept one pain in the ass in – and the BBC bleeped it out for radio.'

Heart Of Glass was released ahead of *Sunday Girl* in most countries, and was promoted with an iconic video directed by Stanley Dorfman. The video included a shot of the famous Studio 54 nightclub, but was actually filmed at a different venue.

Heart Of Glass gave Blondie their biggest hit to date, hitting no.1 in Australia, Austria, Canada, Germany, New Zealand, Switzerland, the UK, the United States and Zimbabwe. The single also achieved no.2 in Ireland and South Africa, no.3 in Sweden, no.4 in Denmark and France, no.8 in Italy and the Netherlands and Norway, no.10 in Spain, no.11 in Finland and no.30 in Japan.

In the UK, where a 7" picture disc single was issued, *Heart Of Glass* is the only Blondie single to top a million copies, and currently stands at around 1.3 million.

Shep Pettibone remixed *Heart Of Glass* for the 1988 album, *ONCE MORE INTO THE BLEACH*. The song was remixed again, this time by Diddy (*aka* Richard Dearlove) for the 1995 compilation, *BEAUTIFUL: THE REMIX ALBUM* ~ this version, released as a single, charted at no.15 in the UK.

The Brazilian supermodel Gisele Bundchen recorded a cover of *Heart Of Glass* with the French producer DJ Bob Sinclair in 2014, as a charity single for the H&M campaign. The single was a Top 40 hit in several European countries, including Belgium, France and Spain, and all proceeds went towards raising funds for UNICEF (United Nations Children's Fund).

9 ~ ONE WAY OR ANOTHER

USA: Chrysalis CHS 2336 (1979).
  B-side: *Just Go Away*.

2.06.79: 69-59-47-41-35-34-41-29-26-**24-24**-27-44-91

UK: not released.

2.03.13: **98**

Canada
22.08.79: peaked at no.**14**, charted for 10 weeks

One Way Or Another was written by Debbie Harry and Nigel Harrison ~ it was inspired by one of Debbie's ex-boyfriends, who had stalked her after they spilt.
  'I broke up with him,' said Debbie, 'and he became a stalker and he was really good at it.'
  One Way Or Another was released as the fourth single from *PARALLEL LINES* in North America only, where it was chosen ahead of *Sunday Girl*. The single achieved no.14 in Canada and no.24 in the United States.
  Although never released as a single, *One Way Or Another* was a minor no.98 hit in the UK in 2013, thanks to digital downloads.

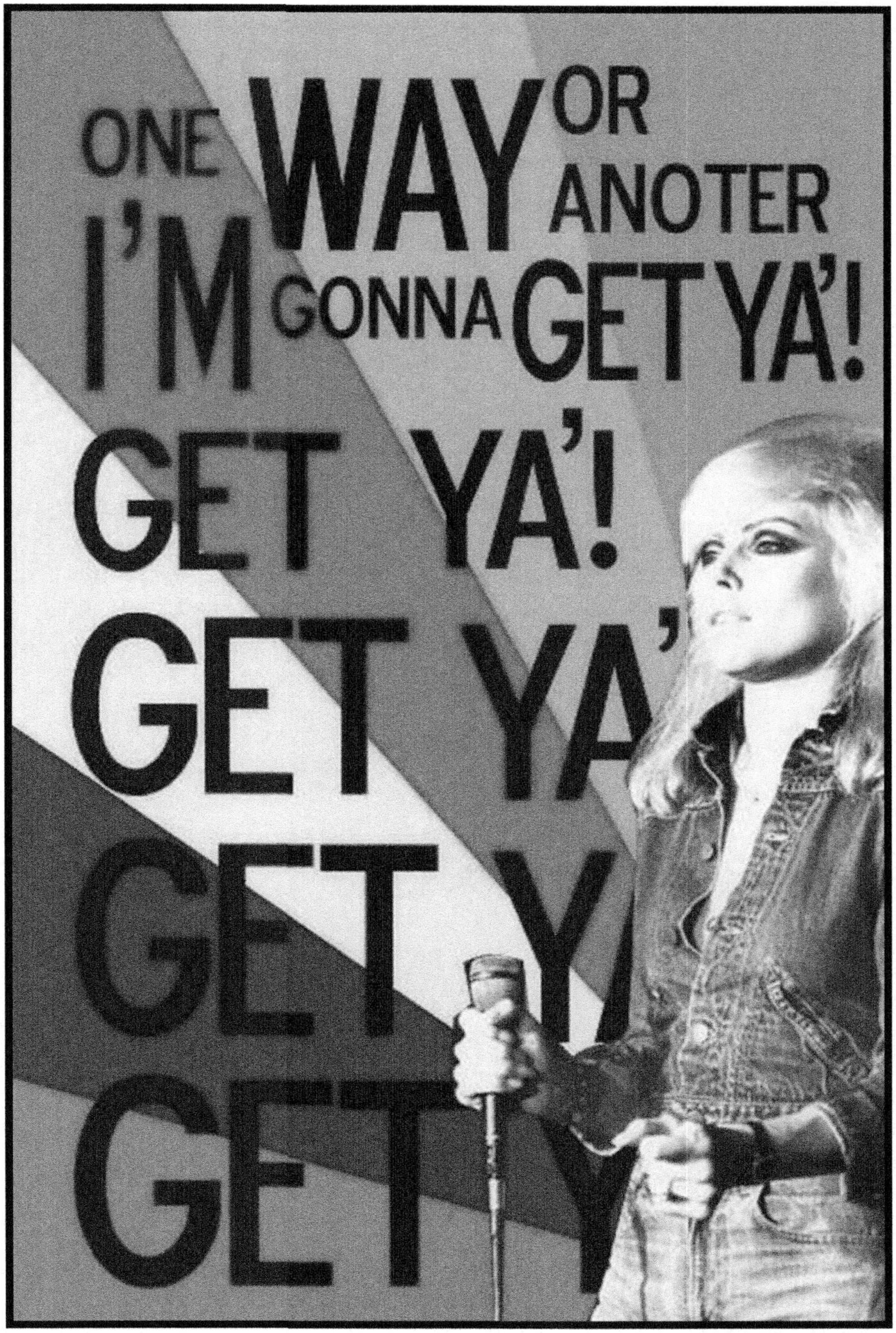
ONE WAY OR ANOTER
I'M GONNA GET YA'!
GET YA'!
GET YA'
GET Y
GET Y

The popular boyband One Direction recorded a cover of *One Way Or Another* in 2013, as a mash-up with the Undertones hit, *Teenage Kicks*.

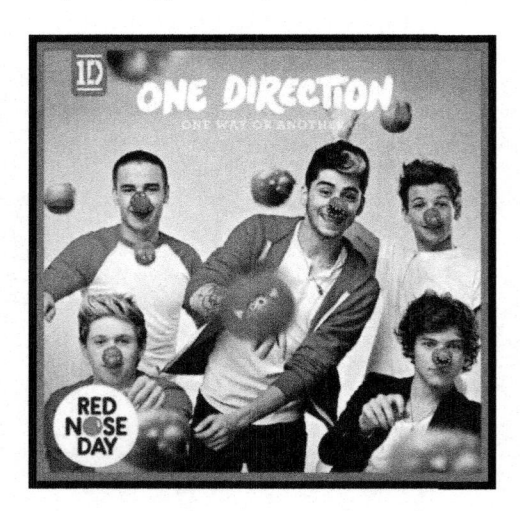

The mash-up was released as a single in support of Comic Relief, and made its debut at no.1 on the UK singles chart. The single also hit no.1 in Denmark, Ireland and the Netherlands, and charted at no.3 in Australia and New Zealand, no.4 in Spain, no.7 in Sweden, no.9 in Canada, no.12 in Austria and Norway, no.13 in the United States, no.15 in Japan, no.17 in France and no.22 in Germany.

10 ~ DREAMING

USA: Chrysalis CHS 2379 (1979).
  B-side: *Living In The Real World*.

29.09.79: 79-69-56-53-42-37-33-30-28-**27**-31-53-97-97

UK: Chrysalis CHS 2350 (1979).
  B-side: *Sound Asleep*.

29.09.79: 7-**2**-3-4-10-13-35-51

Australia
22.10.79: peaked at no.**53**, charted for 8 weeks

Austria
15.11.79: **18** (monthly)

Belgium
20.10.79: 30-21-18-**16**-21-23

Canada
14.11.79: peaked at no.**6**, charted for 18 weeks

Denmark
26.19.79: 9-6-**5-5**

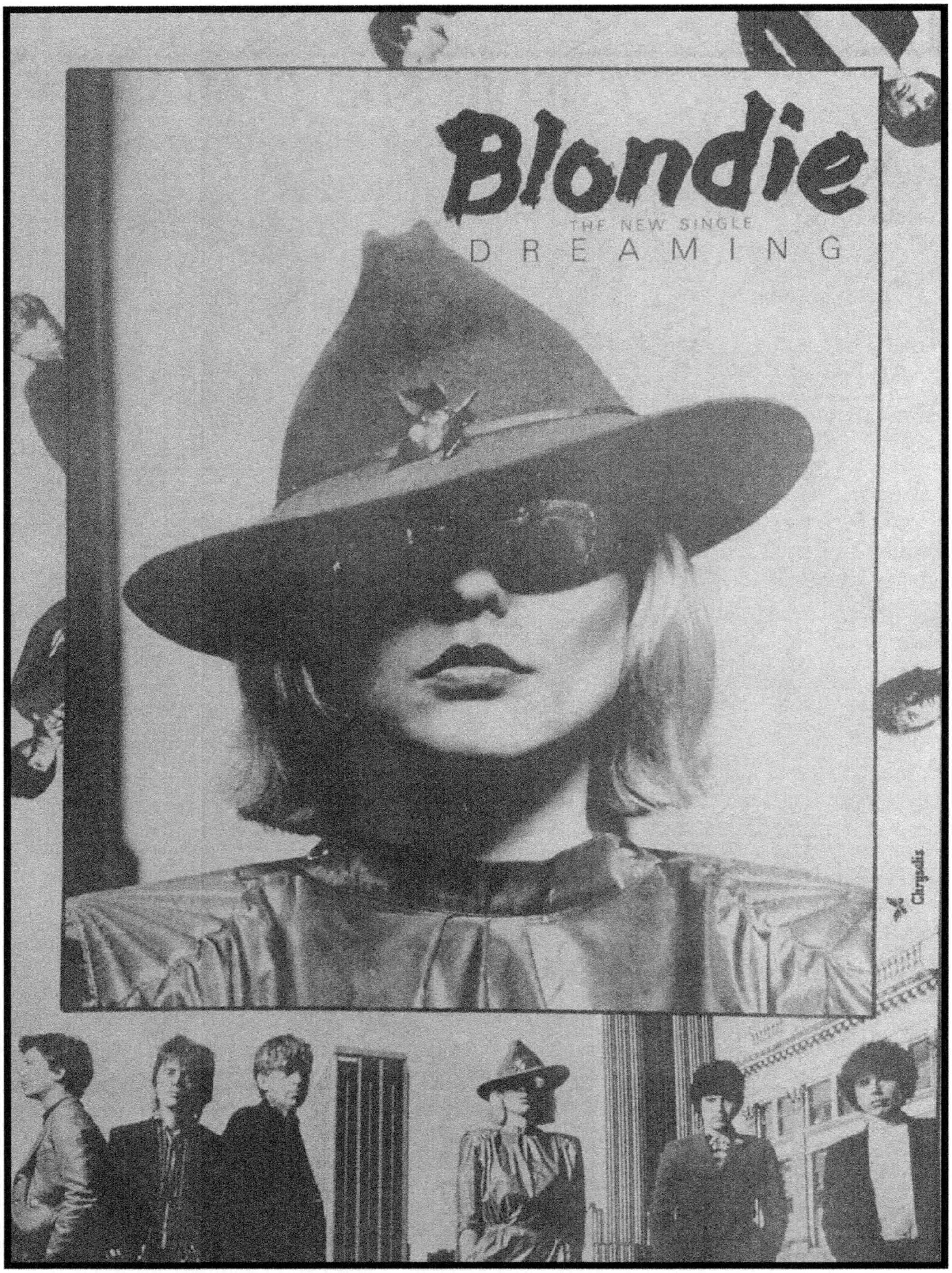
Blondie
THE NEW SINGLE
DREAMING
Chrysalis

Finland
12.79: **20** (monthly)

France
7.09.79: peaked at no.**33**, charted for 15 weeks

Germany
29.10.79: 29-28-**26**-27-32-39-41-45-41-46-61-56-75

Ireland
30.09.79: 12-4-**3**-13-x-x-12-19-17

Netherlands
20.10.79: 31-18-**12**-18-21-33

New Zealand
18.11.79: 15-**9**-**9**-14-**9**-10-10-10-10-25-22-27-26-42-x-44

Norway
10.11.79: 10-7-8-**6**-7-8-9-9

Sweden
2.11.79: **19** (bi-weekly)

Dreaming was written by Debbie Harry and Chris Stein, who later admitted the song was 'pretty much a copy' of ABBA's *Dancing Queen*.

Released as the lead single from Blondie's fourth album, *EAT TO THE BEAT*, *Dreaming* couldn't match the success of *Heart Of Glass*. It achieved no.2 in the UK, no.3 in Ireland, no.5 in Denmark, no.6 in Canada and Norway, no.9 in New Zealand, no.12 in the Netherlands, no.16 in Belgium, no.18 in Austria, no.19 in Sweden, no.20 in Finland, no.26 in Germany and a disappointing no.27 in the United States.

Blondie re-recorded *Dreaming* for their 2014 compilation, *GREATEST HITS DELUXE REDUX*.

11 ~ UNION CITY BLUE

USA: not released.

UK: Chrysalis CHS 2400 (1979).
   B-side: *Living In The Real World*.

24.11.79: 35-21-16-**13**-14-14-16-23-35-59
28.10.95: 31-64 (remix)

Denmark
11.01.80: **9-9**

Germany
7.01.80: **54-54**-58-68-73-72-75-75-70-73

Ireland
2.12.79: 22-**17**-x-28-28-30

New Zealand
17.02.80: 49-x-**47**

Written by Debbie Harry and Nigel Harrison, *Union City Blue* was inspired by the 1980 American crime mystery film, *Union City*, in which Debbie made her acting debut in a starring role as a character called Lillian.

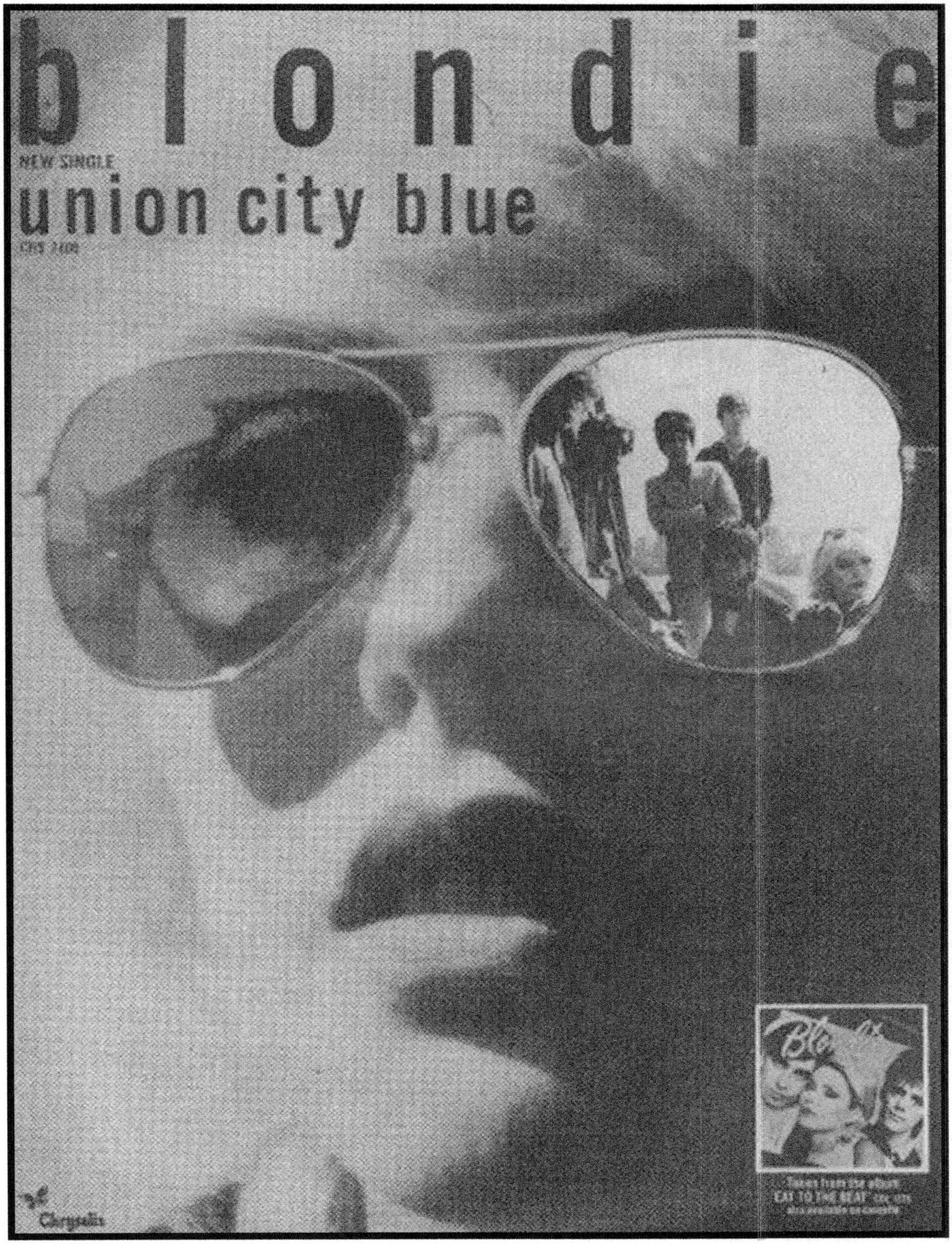
blondie
NEW SINGLE
union city blue

Union City Blue charted at no.9 in Denmark, no.13 in the UK, no.17 in Ireland, no.47 in New Zealand and no.54 in Germany.

In North America, *The Hardest Part* was chosen for single release ahead of *Union City Blue*, but it stalled at no.84 on the Hot 100 in the United States.

Union City Blue was re-released in 1995 as a maxi-single, which featured remixes by Burger Queen, Diddy, Jammin' Hot and OPM. The single charted at no.31 in the UK, and featured Blondie's live version of the Donna Summer hit *I Feel Love* on the B-side, which had previously only been available as a bootleg.

12 ~ CALL ME

USA: Chrysalis CHS 2414 (1980).
 B-side: *Call Me (Instrumental)* (Giorgio Moroder).

16.02.80: 80-70-61-28-12-11-5-3-2-**1-1-1-1-1-1**-2-5-6-12-15-26-33-54-64-98

UK: Chrysalis CHS 2414 (1980).
 B-side: *Call Me (Instrumental)* (Giorgio Moroder).

12.04.80: 21-2-**1**-3-4-14-37-57-61
11.02.89: 69-61-86
15.11.08: 91

Australia
5.05.80: peaked at no.**4**, charted for 20 weeks

Austria
15.06.80: 9-8-6-**5**-6-12 (bi-weekly)

Belgium
10.05.80: 25-19-14-13-11-**9**-10-14

Canada
23.04.80: peaked at no.**1** (6), charted for 17 weeks

He's the highest paid lover in Beverly Hills.
He leaves women feeling more alive than they've ever felt before.
Except one.
American Gigolo
Paramount Pictures Presents A Freddie Fields Production A Film by Paul Schrader Richard Gere in "American Gigolo"
Lauren Hutton Executive Producer Freddie Fields Produced by Jerry Bruckheimer Music Composed by Giorgio Moroder
Written and Directed by Paul Schrader
Original Soundtrack Recording on Polydor Records and Tapes
A Paramount Picture
R
RESTRICTED
Read the Dell Book
"Call Me" performed by Blondie
COPYRIGHT © MCMLXXX
BY PARAMOUNT PICTURES CORPORATION ALL RIGHTS RESERVED
800004

Finland
05.80: peaked at no.**3**, charted for 4 months

France
2.05.80: peaked at no.**4**, charted for 25 weeks

Germany
12.05.80: 18-20-17-**14**-**14**-21-16-18-**14**-**14**-15-22-29-25-36-34-43-51-67-69

Ireland
27.03.80: 7-**2**-13 (bi-weekly)

Italy
31.05.80: peaked at no.**13**, charted for 17 weeks

Japan
5.06.80: peaked at no.**19**, charted for 39 weeks

Netherlands
10.05.80: 21-16-**12**-14-13-16-31-40-44

New Zealand
15.06.80: 7-**6**-**6**-9-11-15-16-23-25-42-42-x-47

Norway
3.05.80: 10-5-5-3-4-5-**2**-**2**-**2**-**2**-5-6-8-7-8

South Africa
5.07.80: peaked at no.**2**, charted for 15 weeks

Sweden
2.05.80: 16-10-5-4-**3**-5-6-7-10-13 (bi-weekly)

Switzerland
11.05.80: 15-9-5-**3**-**3**-**3**-**3**-4-5-4-4-7-10-12-13

Zimbabwe
6.09.80: peaked at no.**3**, charted for 13 weeks

Call Me, which Debbie Harry wrote with the Italian disco producer Giorgio Moroder, was the theme song for the 1980 film, *American Gigolo*, which starred Richard Gere as a male escort.
  Originally, Moroder approached Stevie Nicks from Fleetwood Mac, to ask her to help compose and perform the song, but contractual agreements meant she wasn't able to do so.

Moroder instead turned to Debbie Harry, who was available, and the starting point was an instrumental piece of music titled *Man Machine*. Debbie only took a few hours to come up with the melody and lyrics, saying, 'When I was writing it, I pictured the opening scene, driving on the coast of California.'

Debbie recorded *Call Me* with Blondie, and the band recorded a Spanish language version as well as an English version, titled *Llámame*.

Call Me was hugely successful, and gave Blondie their biggest hit in North America, where it spent six weeks at no.1 in both Canada and the United States. Elsewhere, *Call Me* gave Blondie their fourth no.1 (after *Atomic*) in the UK, and achieved no.2 in Ireland, Norway and South Africa, no.3 in Finland, Sweden, Switzerland and Zimbabwe, no.4 in Australia and France, no.6 in New Zealand, no.9 in Belgium, no.12 in the Netherlands, no.13 in Italy, no.14 in Germany and no.19 in Japan.

Call Me was nominated for a Golden Globe, for Best Original Song, but lost out to Irene Cara's hit, *Fame*. The song was also nominated for a Grammy, for Best Rock Performance by a Duo or Group with Vocals, but once again missed out, the award going to Bob Seger & The Silver Bullet Band's *Against The Wind*.

Although Debbie and Chris Stein were very happy with the success of *Call Me*, the rest of the band regarded the song as too commercial, which led the already strong tensions within the band to increase even further.

Call Me was remixed in 1989 by Ben Liebrand and Bruce Forest & Frank Heller, and released as a single that charted at no.61 in the UK, but wasn't a hit anywhere else.

Blondie re-recorded *Call Me*, again with producer Giorgio Moroder, for their 2014 compilation, *GREATEST HITS DELUXE REDUX*.

13 ~ ATOMIC

USA: Chrysalis CHS 2410 (1980).
  B-side: *Die Young Stay Pretty*.

17.05.80: 71-60-54-47-44-40-40-**39**-92

UK: Chrysalis (1980).
  B-side: *Die Young Stay Pretty*.

23.02.80: 3-**1**-**1**-2-7-18-35-41-46
10.09.94: 19-22-36-53-88 (remix)

Australia
24.03.80: peaked at no.**12**, charted for 22 weeks
?.94: 98 (remix)

Austria
15.04.80: 11-6-**5**-6-16-20 (bi-weekly)

Belgium
23.02.80: 29-15-11-9-**8**-12-16-20-20-14-17-22-25-30

France
25.01.80: peaked at no.**6**, charted for 18 weeks
9.05.98: 84-47-48-55-49-40-25-43-36-40-31-46-54-62-71-73-89 (remix)

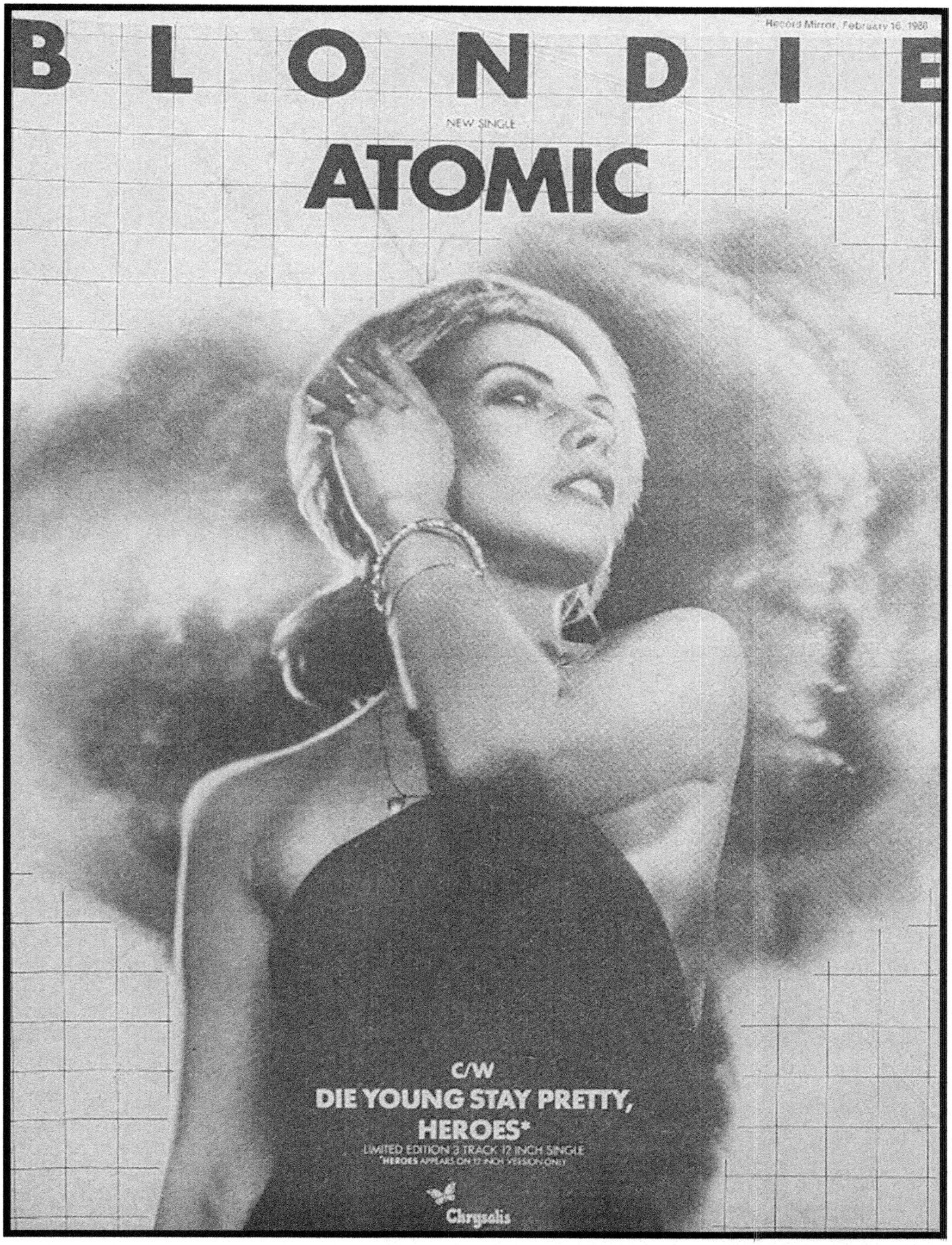
Record Mirror, February 16, 1980
BLONDIE
NEW SINGLE
ATOMIC
C/W
DIE YOUNG STAY PRETTY,
HEROES*
LIMITED EDITION 3 TRACK 12 INCH SINGLE
*HEROES APPEARS ON 12 INCH VERSION ONLY
Chrysalis

Germany
10.03.80: 58-48-25-25-24-**20**-22-29-34-44-51-74-70-47

Ireland
16.03.80: **3**-13 (bi-weekly)

Netherlands
5.04.80: 40-35-**17**-19-22-31-48

New Zealand
20.04.80: 24-21-13-8-**7**-9-10-9-14-13-17-23-28-33-38-42

Norway
8.03.80: 8-x-6-**5-5-5**-6-8-7

South Africa
24.05.80: peaked at no.**16**, charted for 5 weeks

Zimbabwe
10.05.80: peaked at no.**18**, charted for 5 weeks

Atomic was written by Debbie Harry and Jimmy Destri, and was released as the third single from Blondie's *EAT TO THE BEAT* album.

'He (Jimmy) was trying to do something like *Heart Of Glass*,' said Debbie, 'and then somehow or another we gave it the spaghetti western treatment ... a lot of the time I would write while the band were just playing the song and trying to figure it out. I would just be kind of scatting along with them, and I would start going, Ooooooh, your hair is beautiful.'

The intro to *Atomic* was inspired by the popular nursery rhyme *Three Blind Mice*, however, this was edited from the single version of the song, which was also remixed.

Atomic gave Blondie another no.1 in the UK, and the single also charted at no.3 in Ireland, no.5 in Austria and Norway, no.6 in France, no.7 in New Zealand, no.12 in Australia, no.16 in South Africa, no.17 in the Netherlands, no.18 in Zimbabwe, no.20 in Germany and no.39 in the United States.

In the UK, the 12" single featured a live cover of David Bowie's *Heroes*, which had been recorded the previous month at London's Hammersmith Odeon.

Atomic was remixed and reissued in 1994, and returned to the UK chart, peaking at no.19. The following year, the remix topped Billboard's Dance/Club Play chart.

14 ~ THE TIDE IS HIGH

USA: Chrysalis CHS 2465 (1980).
  B-side: *Suzy And Jeffrey*.

15.11.80: 81-58-38-32-20-11-8-8-4-4-3-**1**-2-4-5-7-13-15-27-45-75-82-96-96-99-100

UK: Chrysalis CHS 2465 (1980).
  B-side: *Susie And Jeffrey*.

8.11.80: 5-**1**-**1**-2-2-7-14-20-20-28-47-75

Australia
24.11.80: peaked at no.**4**, charted for 21 weeks

Austria
15.12.80: 11-7-**6**-7-8-12-17 (bi-weekly)

Belgium
15.11.80: 30-17-13-7-**4**-6-9-10-18-22-32

Canada
31.01.81: peaked at no.**1** (4), charted for 16 weeks

Denmark
12.12.80: 6-**4**-**4**-**4**-5-7-9-8-9-9

BLONDIE
'...THE TIDE IS HIGH
BUT I'M HOLDING ON
I'M GONNA BE YOUR No 1'
NEW SINGLE
THE TIDE IS HIGH
TAKEN FROM THE FORTHCOMING ALBUM
'AUTOAMERICAN'
Chrysalis

Finland
01.81: **19** (monthly)

France
14.11.80: peaked at no.**31**, charted for 16 weeks

Germany
24.11.80: 50-24-19-**15**-18-22-29-28-21-19-24-22-26-31-37-40-56-66-62

Ireland
16.11.80: 4-**2-2-2**-5-12-19-19-19-22-30

Italy
27.12.80: peaked at no.**16**, charted for 4 weeks

Japan
1.12.80: peaked at no.**68**, charted for 8 weeks

Netherlands
15.11.80: 13-7-7-7-**5**-12-8-23-26-48

New Zealand
18.01.81: 3-2-2-2-**1-1**-3-2-4-9-27-35-33-40

Norway
29.11.80: 10-9-**7**

South Africa
3.01.81: peaked at no.**5**, charted for 12 weeks

Sweden
26.12.80: **19** (bi-weekly)

Switzerland
7.12.80: 15-9-6-**5-5-5-5**-9-11-13

Zimbabwe
7.03.81: peaked at no.**8**, charted for 11 weeks

The Tide Is High was written by John Holt, who recorded the original version of the song with the Jamaican reggae group The Paragons in 1966, for their album *ON THE BEACH*. *The Tide Is High* was released as a single in Jamaica, while in the UK it was issued as the B-side of *Only A Smile*.

THE TIDE IS HIGH

Recorded by **BLONDIE** on CHRYSALIS Records

Words and Music by JOHN HOLT

THE SPARTA FLORIDA MUSIC GROUP LTD.

chappell

Blondie recorded a cover of *The Tide Is High* for their fifth studio album, *AUTOAMERICAN*, released in 1980. The track was chosen as the album's lead single, and gave Blondie their third no.1 single on the Hot 100 in the United States, and their fifth no.1 in the UK.

Elsewhere, *The Tide Is High* hit no.1 in Canada and New Zealand, and charted at no.2 in Ireland, no.4 in Australia, Belgium and Denmark, no.5 in the Netherlands, South Africa and Switzerland, no.6 in Austria, no.7 in Norway, no.8 in Zimbabwe, no.15 in Germany, no.16 in Italy, no.19 in Finland and Sweden and no.31 in France.

Numerous acts have recorded versions of *The Tide Is High* over the years. Papa Dee, a Swedish rap/ragga artist, recorded a cover for his 1996 album, *THE JOURNEY*, which as a single achieved Top 20 status in Finland.

Blondie apart, the most successful cover of *The Tide Is High* was recorded by the British female trio Atomic Kitten, for their 2002 album, *FEELS SO GOOD*. Thanks to a new bridge added to the song, their cover was sub-titled 'Get The Feeling'.

Released as the second single from the album, Atomic Kitten took their version of *The Tide Is High* to no.1 in Ireland, New Zealand and the UK, and into the Top 5 in numerous other countries, including Australia, Austria, Germany, the Netherlands, Sweden and Switzerland.

15 ~ RAPTURE

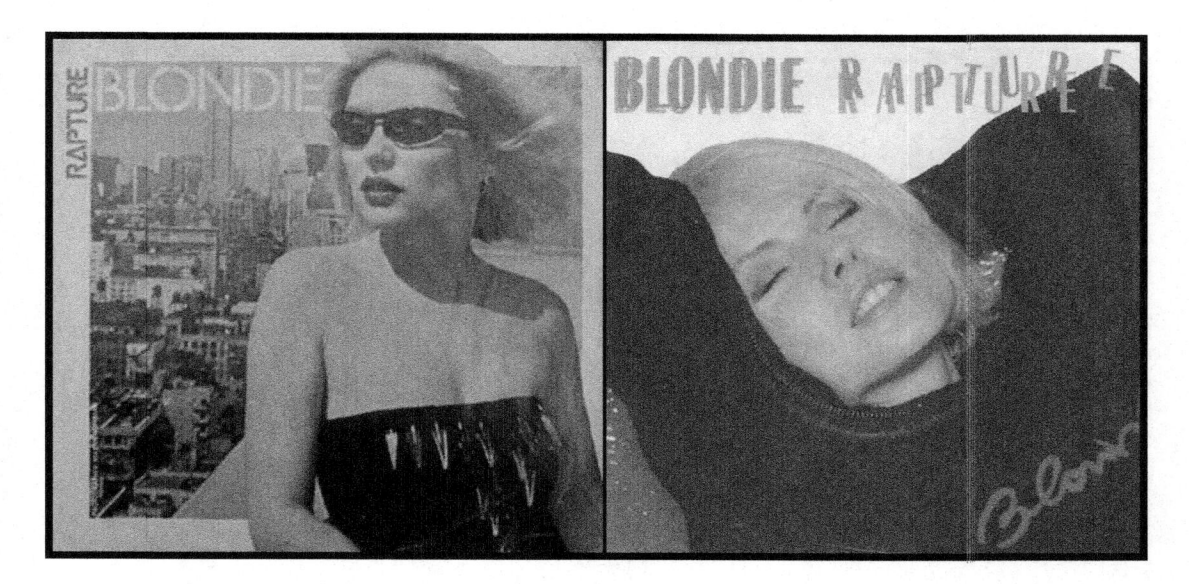

USA: Chrysalis CHS 2485 (1981).
  B-side: *Walk Like Me.*

31.01.81: 61-42-32-19-15-12-7-6-**1-1**-2-2-6-6-14-31-52-75-93-100

UK: Chrysalis CHS 2485 (1981).
  B-side: *Walk Like Me.*

24.01.81: 14-**5-5**-8-13-27-36-61

Australia
16.03.81: peaked at no.**5**, charted for 15 weeks

Belgium
14.02.81: 31-19-16-**8**-12-15-20-24-40

Canada
4.04.81: peaked at no.**1** (3), charted for 12 weeks

France
2.01.81: peaked at no.**30**, charted for 6 weeks

Germany
23.02.81: **40**-48-48-47-52-56-61-60-63-74-66-69-71

RAPTURE
Words by DEBORAH HARRY
Music by CHRIS STEIN
Recorded by BLONDIE on CHRYSALIS Records
RARE BLUE MUSIC, INC./MONSTER ISLAND MUSIC

Ireland
1.02.81: 18-7-**4**-8-27

Italy
7.02.81: peaked at no.**25**, charted for 2 weeks

Netherlands
14.02.81: 37-**20**-29-33-35-40

New Zealand
12.04.81: 8-**4**-8-13-13-19-25-43

SHEER RAPTURE

THE NEW BLONDIE ALBUM, WITH 132 PAGE MAGAZINE, CLASSIC PIN BADGES, GIANT POSTER AND EXCLUSIVE POSTCARDS

AVAILABLE FROM
www.myfavouritemagazines.co.uk
and all good newsagents

Norway
28.02.81: 9-**8**-9-9

South Africa
21.03.81: peaked at no.**6**, charted for 8 weeks

Spain
18.05.81: peaked at no.**21**, charted for 5 weeks

Sweden
27.03.81: **13**-20 (bi-weekly)

Zimbabwe
23.05.81: peaked at no.7, charted for 5 weeks

Rapture was written by Debbie Harry & Chris Stein, and recorded by Blondie for their 1980 album, *AUTOAMERICAN*. It was the second and final single released from the album, and gave Blondie their fourth and last no.1 on the Hot 100 in the United States, where it was the first chart topper to feature rap vocals (by Debbie).

Rapture was also the first music video to feature rap vocals to be shown on MTV. The song's lyrics name-checked rappers Grandmaster Flash and Fab Five Freddy, both of whom were scheduled to make a cameo appearance in the promo, but only Fab Five Freddy actually turned up for filming.

Outside the United States, *Rapture* hit no.1 in Canada, and achieved no.4 in Ireland and New Zealand, no.5 in Australia and the UK, no.6 in South Africa, no.7 in Zimbabwe, no.8 in Belgium and Norway, no.13 in Sweden, no.20 in the Netherlands, no.21 in Spain, no.25 in Italy, no.30 in France and no.49 in Germany.

In 2005, *Rapture* was released as a mash-up with *Riders On The Storm* by The Doors, titled *Rapture Riders*. Credited to Blondie vs. The Doors, *Rapture Riders* became a Top 40 hit in its own right (see later entry).

Blondie re-recorded *Rapture* in 2014, for the compilation album, *GREATEST HITS DELUXE REDUX*.

Grandmaster Flash released a scratch mix version of *Rapture* in 1988, titled *The Adventures Of Grandmaster Flash On The Wheels Of Steel*.

Erasure recorded a cover of *Rapture* for their 1997 album, *COWBOY*, but it was only released on the North American edition of the album. Alicia Keys also recorded a cover of *Rapture*, which featured on the 2010 soundtrack album, *SEX AND THE CITY 2*.

16 ~ BACKFIRED

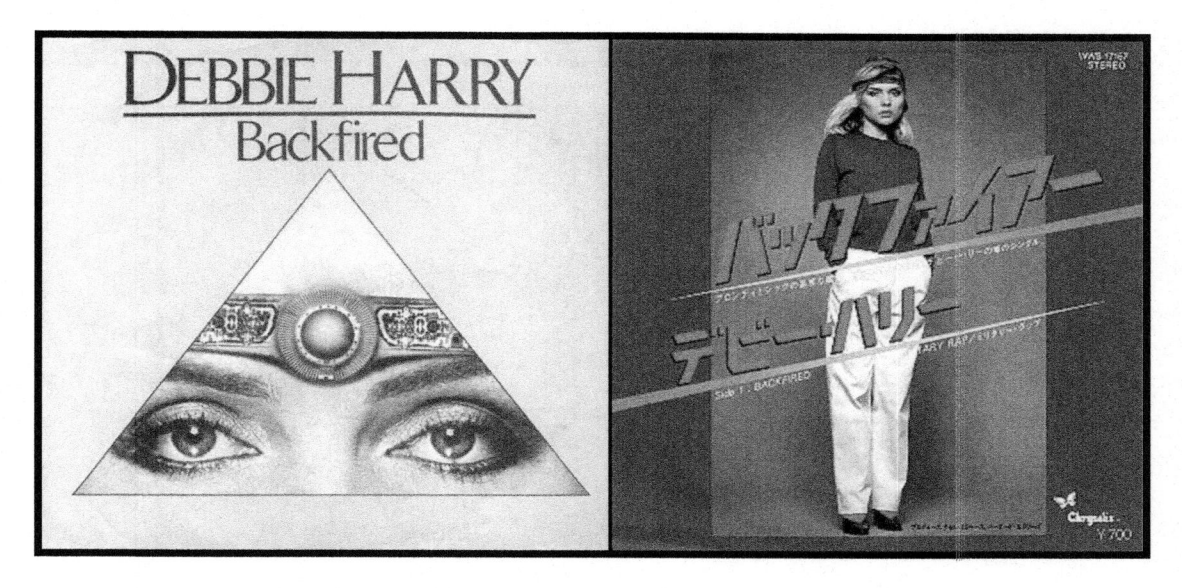

USA: Chrysalis CHS 2526 (1981).
  B-side: *Military Rap*.

15.08.81: 75-65-55-48-44-**43**-47-57-62-92

UK: Chrysalis CHS2526 (1981).
  B-side: *Military Rap*.

1.08.81: 49-**32**-36-40-59-75

Australia
7.09.81: peaked at no.**23**, charted for 10 weeks

Italy
10.10.81: **24**

New Zealand
11.10.81: 30-33-31-**28**-42

Sweden
28.08.81: **16** (bi-weekly)

Backfired was the lead single from Debbie's debut solo album, *KOOKOO*. The song was written and produced by Nile Rodgers and Bernard Edwards, who co-founded the very successful dance band, Chic.

DEBBIE HARRY
Backfired

c/w Military Rap

A SINGLE PRODUCED BY NILE ROGERS AND BERNARD EDWARDS
FOR THE CHIC ORGANISATION LTD
TAKEN FROM THE FORTHCOMING ALBUM
Koo Koo

In an effort to establish herself as a solo artist, and distance herself from Blondie, Debbie changed her image and dyed her hair darker. However, *Backfired* proved less popular than many of Blondie's singles, charting at no.16 in Sweden, no.23 in Australia, no.24 in Italy, no.28 in New Zealand, no.32 in the UK and a disappointing no.43 in the United States.

The Jam Was Moving, the second single lifted from *KOOKOO* in most countries, was a minor hit in the United States, but it bombed everywhere else.

N° 176 septembre 81 9 F mensuel
rock & folk
BLONDIE
ROXY MUSIC
ROLLING STONES
ELVIS PRESLEY
COUNTRY ROCK
TOOTS
2531 - 176 - 9 F 4,30 FS
DEBORAH HARRY

17 ~ ISLAND OF LOST SOULS

USA: Chrysalis CHS 2603 (1982).
   B-side: *Dragonfly*.

29.05.82: 66-54-49-41-39-**37-37**-53-70-95

UK: Chrysalis CHS 2608 (1982).
   B-side: *Dragonfly*.

8.05.82: 39-24-21-14-12-**11**-20-30-62

Australia
7.06.82: peaked at no.**13**, charted for 15 weeks

Belgium
29.05.82: 26-14-**8**-12-27

France
7.05.82: peaked at no.**45**, charted for 18 weeks

Germany
7.06.82: 71-**66**-71-73

Ireland
23.05.82: 19-**15**-18-18-18-25

THE NEW SINGLE FROM
BLONDIE
ISLAND OF LOST SOULS
CHS 2608
B/W DRAGONFLY
FROM THE FORTHCOMING ALBUM "THE HUNTER" – PRODUCED BY MIKE CHAPMAN
LIMITED EDITION PICTURE DISC
ALSO 7" IN FULL COLOUR BAG
CHSP 2608
Chrysalis

Netherlands
22.05.82: 27-25-29-**21**-38

New Zealand
18.07.82: 39-28-30-19-**18**-22-35-33-38-44

Zimbabwe
7.08.82: **20**

Island Of Lost Souls, composed by Deborah Harry & Chris Stein, was the lead single from Blondie's sixth studio album, *THE HUNTER*, released in 1982.

The calypso feel of *Island Of Lost Souls* was completely different from the group's previous single, *Rapture*, and proved much less successful. The single only just achieved Top 40 status in the United States, where is stalled at no.37.

Elsewhere, *Island Of Lost Souls* charted at no.8 in Belgium, no.11 in the UK, no.13 in Australia, no.15 in Ireland, no.18 in New Zealand, no.20 in Zimbabwe, no.21 in the Netherlands and no.45 in France.

CIAO 2001
13 GIUGNO 1982 - N. 24 - ANNO XIV - L. 800
BOWIE
GENESIS
RY COODER
BLONDIE

18 ~ WAR CHILD

USA: not released.

UK: Chrysalis CHS 2624 (1982).
  B-side: *Little Caesar*.

17.07.82: 98-56-**39**-44-66

Australia
13.09.82: peaked at no.**96**, charted for 2 weeks

Ireland
8.08.82: 22-**21**

Outside North America, the second and last single released from *THE HUNTER* album was *War Child*, which was written by Debbie Harry and Nigel Harrison. The lyrics touched on wars in Cambodia and the Middle East, but *War Child* proved even less successful than *Island Of Lost Souls*, charting at no.21 in Ireland, no.39 in the UK and a lowly no.96 in Australia.

War Child was Blondie's last new single for 17 years, until the group reformed and returned to the chart in 1999, with *Maria*.

BLONDIE
WAR CHILD

NEW SINGLE ON 7" AND 12" VERSIONS

12" EXTENDED VERSION 8.02 MINS   Chrysalis   TAKEN FROM THE ALBUM 'THE HUNTER'

19 ~ RUSH RUSH

USA: Chrysalis VS4 42745 (1983).
 B-side: *Dance, Dance, Dance* (Beth Anderson).

Rush Rush failed to enter the Hot 100 in the United States, but it did spend a week at no.5 on the 'Bubbling Under' chart.

UK: Chrysalis CHS 2752 (1984).
 B-side: *Rush Rush (Dub Mix)*.

11.02.84: 96-**94**-87

Australia
19.03.84: peaked at no.**25**, charted for 17 weeks

New Zealand
6.05.84: **39**

Debbie recorded *Rush Rush* for the soundtrack to the 1983 American crime movie, *Scarface*, which starred Al Pacino as a Cuban refugee, Tony 'Scarface' Montana, who comes to the United States and becomes a drugs king.
 Rush Rush, together with all the songs featured on the *SCARFACE* original soundtrack album, was composed and produced by Giorgio Moroder, best known for his work with Donna Summer.

AL PACINO SCARFACE

In the spring of 1980, the port at Mariel Harbor was opened, and thousands set sail for the United States. They came in search of the American Dream.

One of them found it on the sun-washed avenues of Miami...wealth, power and passion beyond his dreams.

He loved the American Dream. with a vengeance.

He was Tony Montana. the world will remember him by another name ...SCARFACE.

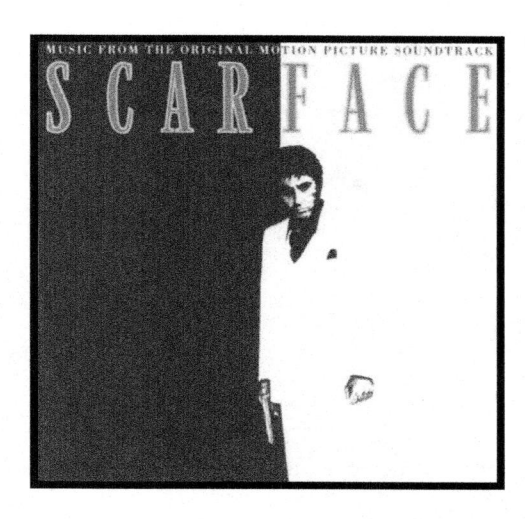

Rush Rush achieved Top 40 status in two countries, peaking at no.25 in Australia and no.39 in New Zealand. It was a minor hit in the UK, but failed to enter the Hot 100 in the United States, and didn't chart in most countries.

Debbie followed *Rush Rush* with *Feel The Spin*, which she recorded for the soundtrack of the 1985 film, *KRUSH GROOVE*.

Debbie co-wrote *Feel The Spin* with John 'Jellybean' Benitez and Tony C. ~ it was released as a single in North America only, but it wasn't a hit.

20 ~ FRENCH KISSIN

USA: Geffen Records 7-28546 (1986).
  B-side: *Rockbird*.

22.11.86: 98-91-73-69-64-61-61-**57**-60-62-94

UK: Chrysalis CHS 3066 (1986).
  B-side: *Rockbird*.

15.11.86: 27-11-9-**8**-11-14-19-19-22-53

Australia
22.12.86: peaked at no.**4**, charted for 21 weeks

Belgium
6.12.86: 37-25-19-17-16-**15**-16-25-28-40

Germany
26.01.87: 50-43-**28**-29-31-41-58-58-69-72

Ireland
23.11.86: 9-**8**-11-18-18

Netherlands
20.12.86: 47-**32**-37-40-40-43

DEBBIE HARRY

FRENCH KISSIN

New 7 & 12" Single
FROM THE FORTHCOMING ALBUM
'ROCKBIRD'

Chrysalis

HEAR IT NOW
ON YOUR PHONE
0898 600-190

New Zealand
1.02.87: 13-6-3-**2**-5-9-10-7-14-12-27-28

South Africa
22.03.87: peaked at no.**8**, charted for 6 weeks

French Kissin, also known as *French Kissin In The USA*, was composed by Chuck Lorre, and recorded by Debbie for her second solo album, *ROCKBIRD*. It was released as the album's lead single, and gave Debbie her biggest solo hit to date, charting at no.2 in New Zealand, no.4 in Australia, no.8 in Ireland and the UK, no.15 in Belgium, no.28 in Germany, no.32 in the Netherlands and no.57 in the United States.

French Kissin was released as a limited edition 12" picture disc single in the UK.

Debbie recorded a French version of *French Kissin*, which featured as the B-side of the follow-up, *In Love With Love*, in some countries. *In Love With Love* failed to achieve Top 40 status anywhere.

21 ~ I WANT THAT MAN

USA: Sire 7-22816 (1989).
  B-side: *Bike Boy (CD/Cassette Version)*.

I Want That Man wasn't a hit in the United States.

UK: Chrysalis CHS 3369 (1989).
  B-side: *Bike Boy*.

7.10.89: 52-36-21-14-**13**-15-16-25-40-67

Australia
20.11.89: peaked at no.**2**, charted for 26 weeks
02.00: 86 (remix)

Belgium
25.11.89: **48**

Ireland
15.10.89: 29-17-**7**-8-16-x-30

New Zealand
11.02.90: 46-x-48-17-14-11-**8**-24-29-28-34-41-x-45

I Want That Man, the lead single from her third solo album, *DEF DUMB & BLONDE*, saw Debbie Harry changing the name most people knew her by to the more mature sounding Deborah Harry.

I Want That Man was composed by Alannah Currie and Tom Bailey of the Thompson Twins, and was inspired by the actor Harry Dean Stanton. Outside North America, the single was one of Deborah's most successful, peaking at no.2 in Australia, no.7 in Ireland, no.8 in New Zealand, no.13 in the UK and no.48 in Belgium.

The original, together with two remixed versions, of *I Want That Man* featured on the 1999 compilation, *MOST OF ALL – THE BEST OF*.

22 ~ SWEET AND LOW

USA: Sire/Red Eye/Reprise Records 9 21492-2 (1989).
Tracks: *Sweet And Low (Single Version)/(LP Edit)/(Phil Harding 12" Mix)/Lovelight (LP Version)/Sweet And Low (Sweet House Mix)/(Swing Low Mix)*.

Sweet And Low wasn't a hit in the United States.

UK: Chrysalis CHS 3491 (1990).
B-side: *Lovelight*.

31.03.90: 59-**57**-69

Australia
26.02.90: peaked at no.**31**, charted for 13 weeks.

Deborah co-wrote *Sweet And Low* with Chris Stein and Toni C, and recorded it for her album, *DEF DUMB & BLONDE*. In the UK, it was released as the album's third single, following *Brite Side*, which failed to achieve Top 40 status anywhere. The single charted at no.57, a two place improvement on the position achieved by *Brite Side*.

In Australia, *Sweet And Low* was issued as a double A-side with *Kiss It Better*, and rose as high as no.31 during a three month chart run.

Sweet And Low failed to enter the Hot 100 in the United States, but it did achieve no.17 on Billboard's Dance Chart.

Sweet And Low was released as a 12" picture disc single in the UK only.

23 ~ WELL, DID YOU EVAH!

USA: not released.

UK: Chrysalis 3646 (1990).
   B-side: *Who Wants To Be A Millionaire?* (The Thompson Twins).

5.01.91: 70-49-**42**-52

Ireland
20.01.91: **29**

Well, Did You Evah! was composed by Cole Porter, for his 1939 musical, *DuBarry Was A Lady*. In the original production, the song was introduced by Betty Grable and Charles Walters.
   The best known version of *Well, Did You Evah!* was performed by Bing Crosby and Frank Sinatra, in the 1956 musical, *High Society*.

Deborah recorded *Well, Did You Evah!* with former punk rocker Iggy Pop, for the 1990 compilation album, *RED HOT + BLUE*. The album was released as a tribute to Cole Porter, and benefited HIV/AIDS research and relief.

Well, Did You Evah! charted at no.29 in Ireland and no.42 in the UK, where the single was released as a limited edition 12" picture disc.

24 ~ I CAN SEE CLEARLY

USA: Sire/Reprise Records 9 41000-2 (1993).
   Tracks: *I Can See Clearly (Single Version)/(The Club Mix)/(Boriqua Tribal Mix)/(Blonde Rave)/(Dub-A-Mental)/(Hot Single Mix)/(N.Y.C. Dub)*.

I Can See Clearly wasn't a hit in the United States.

UK: Chrysalis CDCHSS 4900 (1993).
   Tracks: *I Can See Clearly/Atomic/Heart Of Glass*.

3.07.93: **23**-28-47-66

Australia
09.93: **96**

I Can See Clearly was written by Arthur Baker and Tony McIlwaine, and recorded by Deborah for her fourth solo album, *DEBRAVATION*. It was chosen as the album's lead single, and owes its Top 40 status to the no.23 debut position it achieved in the UK.
   I Can See Clearly was a minor hit in Australia and, although it failed to enter the Hot 100, the single did rise to no.2 on Billboard's Dance Chart in the United States.

the new single
deborah harry
i can see clearly
12" contains d:reamix & murk habana dub
tc contains standing in my way with joey ramone
cd1 contains classic tracks atomic & heart of glass
cd2 contains call me & in love with love (out next week)
out now
Chrysalis

25 ~ MARIA

USA: Logic Records/Beyond 74321-78040-2 (1999).
Tracks: *Maria (Soul Solution Full Remix)/(Talvin Singh Remix)/(Talvin Singh Rhythmic Remix Edit)/(Album Version)*.

10.04.99: **82**-92-96-98-94-94

UK: Beyond 7432164563 2 (1999).
Tracks: *Maria (Radio Edit)/(Soul Solution Remix Radio Edit)/(Talvin Singh Remix Edit)*.

13.02.99: **1**-2-6-11-15-19-26-30-41-45-48-56-91-90-86-90-x-x-100-84

Australia
02.99: peaked at no.**59**

Austria
21.03.99: 23-16-7-5-4-**2**-4-4-5-6-13-11-14-17-26-32

Belgium
6.03.99: 46-30-19-9-5-**3-3**-6-8-9-7-9-12-13-19-27-32-43

France
20.02.99: 62-33-**31**-43-41-43-46-49-53-54-52-60-60-71-81-88-96-99

Germany
8.02.99: 91-73-57-33-19-12-6-4-**3-3**-5-5-5-5-6-6-7-8-11-18-26-34-47-53-58

Ireland
4.02.99: 11-7-4-**3**-7-8-10-15-30

Italy
17.04.99: peaked at no.**15**, charted for 9 weeks

Netherlands
13.03.99: 87-66-46-35-31-25-22-20-20-21-**19-19**-22-24-28-38-49-55-61-71-85

New Zealand
7.03.99: 22-19-**16**-26-36-22-23-47-49-44

Spain
13.03.99: 3-2-4-11-**1**-5-3-4-3-4-7-8-14-14

Sweden
4.03.99: 50-44-37-25-26-27-27-11-8-10-11-**7**-10-10-11-15-21-24-29-30-56-40-38-42

Switzerland
7.02.99: 45-29-44-20-12-11-9-7-**3**-6-6-4-7-9-11-14-15-21-24-26-35-45-43-41-42-42-40

After an absence of nearly 17 years, Blondie reformed and returned with their seventh studio album, *NO EXIT*. Written by the band's keyboard player, Jimmy Destri, *Maria* was chosen as the album's lead single ~ it was Blondie's first new single since *War Child* in 1982.

'*Maria* wasn't my choice for the first single off the new album,' said Deborah Harry, 'I would have chosen a much bigger song, not such a simple pop song.'

In the UK, *Maria* was released as a 2CD set, one CD featuring remixes of *Maria* and the second CD including live versions of the band's debut single, *In The Flesh*, and *Screaming Skin* (from *NO EXIT*), both recorded during Blondie's No Exit Tour.

Maria made its chart debut at no.1 in the UK, to give Blondie their sixth chart topper, and their first since 1980. The single also went to no.1 in Spain, and charted at no.2 in Austria, no.3 in Belgium, Germany, Ireland and Switzerland, no.7 in Sweden, no.15 in Italy, no.16 in New Zealand, no.19 in the Netherlands, no31 in France, no.59 in Australia and a lowly no.82 in the United States.

26 ~ NOTHING IS REAL BUT THE GIRL

USA: BMG BYDJ-78042 (promo, 1999).
Tracks: *Nothing Is Real But The Girl (Radio Remix)/(Radio Remix with Alternate Intro)*.

Nothing Is Real But The Girl wasn't a hit in the United States.

UK: Beyond 74321 66380 2 (1999).
Tracks: *Nothing Is Real But The Girl (Boilerhouse Mix)/(Danny Tenaglia Club Mix)/ (Danny Tenaglia Instradub)*.

12.06.99: **26**-53-62-89

Germany
12.07.99: 99-x-**89**-96-93

Spain
29.05.99: **11**-15-18

Like *Maria*, *Nothing Is Real But The Girl* was written by Jimmy Destri, originally with his daughter in mind.
'It's about his daughter,' Deborah Harry confirmed. 'It's about the hard times he went through and watching his little girl. Nothing mattered but her. It's very sweet, too.'
However, for single release, Blondie re-recorded the song with altered lyrics, to shift the focus from the third to first person, so focusing on the band's lead singer, Deborah.
Released as the follow-up to *Maria*, *Nothing Is Real But The Girl* was once again issued as a 2CD set in the UK. The first CD featured three remixes of *Nothing Is Real But The Girl*, and the

second CD included live versions of *Maria* and *Rip Her To Shreds*, recorded in November 1998 during concerts in London and Glasgow, respectively.

Nothing Is Real But The Girl couldn't match the success of *Maria*, and interestingly it performed best in the two countries where *Maria* had topped the chart, rising to no.11 in Spain and no.26 in the UK. The single was also a minor hit in Germany, but it failed to chart in most countries.

The title track of *NO EXIT* was released as a single in Europe only, but it failed to enter the charts anywhere.

27 ~ GOOD BOYS

USA: Sanctuary Records SANDJ-85600-2 (promo, 2003).
   Tracks: *Good Boys (Radio Edit)/(Album Version)*.

Good Boys wasn't a hit in the United States.

UK: Epic 674399 2 (2003).
   Tracks: *Good Boys (Album Version)/Maria (Live)/Rapture (Live)/Good Boys (Video – B&W Version/Colour)*.

18.10.03: **12**-24-50-x-x-85-84

Australia
24.08.03: **37**-55-79-81

Germany
20.10.03: **93**

Good Boys was the only single released from Blondie's eighth studio album, *THE CURSE OF BLONDIE*.
   The track was written by Deborah Harry and Kevin Griffin, but … some of the lyrics caused controversy, as they were very similar to three lines from Queen's *We Will Rock You*.
   Good Boys included the lyrics:

You got me on your face
A big disgrace

Shakin' your feathers all over the place

While *We Will Rock You* featured:

*You got mud on your face
You big disgrace
Kicking your can all over the place*

Queen threatened to sue, and as a result all subsequent pressings of *Good Boys* credited Queen's Brian May, who composed *We Will Rock You*, as one of the song's co-writers.

Good Boys charted at no.12 in the UK and no.37 in Australia, and was a minor hit in Germany, but it failed to chart in most countries. In the UK, a 2CD set was released, with one CD including live versions of *Maria* and *Rapture*, while the second CD featured remixes by Giorgio Moroder. A 12" single was also released, with remixes by Moroder, Arthur Baker and the Scissor Sisters.

In Japan, *Good Boys* was issued as a promo 12" picture disc single.

There was an eight year gap between *Good Boys* and Blondie's next single, *Mother*, which was chosen as the lead single from the album *PANIC OF GIRLS* ~ it wasn't a hit.

28 ~ RAPTURE RIDERS

USA: Capitol Records DPRO 0946 3 56426 2 9 (promo, 2006).
 Tracks: *Rapture Riders (Single Edit)/(Full Version)/Rapture (Special Disco Mix)*.

Rapture Riders wasn't a hit in the United States.

UK: EMI/Virgin (promo, 2005).
 Tracks: *Rapture Riders (Single Edit)/(Full Version)*.

Rapture Riders wasn't a hit in the UK.

Australia
14.05.06: **23**-37-35-31-33-45-48-56-63-84-84-72-77-85-85

Belgium
25.03.06: 29-23-**21**-22-28-33-36-40-48-49

Finland
15.04.06: **12**-14

Netherlands
11.03.06: 40-**39**-48-47-x-x-92

Rapture Riders started life as an unofficial 'mash-up' of two songs, Blondie's *Rapture* and *Riders On The Storm*, a 1971 hit for The Doors.

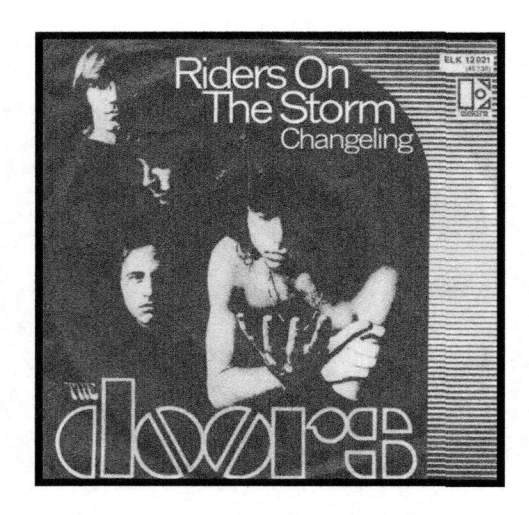

After both bands approved the mash-up, *Rapture Riders* was officially released as a single, credited to Blondie vs. The Doors. The single achieved no.12 in Finland, no.21 in Belgium, no.23 in Australia and no.39 in the Netherlands.

In the United States, although it failed to enter the Hot 100, *Rapture Riders* did climb to no.10 on Billboard's Hot Dance Club Play chart.

Rapture Riders was included on Blondie's 2005 compilation, *GREATEST HITS: SIGHT + SOUND*.

29 ~ NEW YORK, NEW YORK

USA: not released.

UK: Mute CDMute371 (2006).
   Tracks: *New York, New York (Single Version)/Go (Trentemoller Remix Edit)* (Moby).

4.11.06: 83-**43**-85

Austria
10.11.06: 53-**47**-54-68-75

Belgium
11.11.06: **38**-41-47-**38**-43-43-50

Germany
10.11.06: **69**-89-83-92

Italy
26.10.06: 19-**17**

Netherlands
11.11.06: 67-**64**-91-x-100

Switzerland
19.11.06: **80**-86

Moby (*aka* Richard Melville Hall) wrote and produced *New York, New York* for his 2006 compilation, *GO – THE VERY BEST OF MOBY*. The track was credited to Moby featuring Debbie Harry.

New York, New York charted at no.17 in Italy, no.38 in Belgium, no.39 in Ireland, no.43 in the UK and no.47 in Austria, and was a minor hit in Germany, the Netherlands and Switzerland.

THE ALMOST TOP 40 SINGLES

No Blondie singles have made the Top 50 in one or more countries, but failed to enter the Top 40 in any, but three solo singles by Debbie/Deborah Harry have ~ as has a medley of Blondie hits by This Year's Blonde.

Free To Fall

Debbie co-wrote *Free To Fall* with Seth Justman, and recorded it for her 1986 album, *ROCKBIRD*. It was released as the second single from the album, after *French Kissin'*, but the only country where it charted was the UK, where it peaked at no.46.

In Love With Love

Like *Free To Fall*, Debbie recorded *In Love With Love* for her 1986 album, *ROCKBIRD*. She co-wrote the song with Chris Stein, and it was released as the follow-up to *Free To Fall*. But, like *Free To Fall*, the only country where the single came close to achieving Top 40 status was the UK, where it charted at no.45. *In Love With Love* was also a minor no.70 on the Hot 100 in the United States, but it didn't chart anywhere else.

Strike Me Pink

Deborah co-wrote *Strike Me Pink* with Anne Dudley and Jonathan Bernstein, and recorded it for her 1993 album, *DEBRAVATION*. It was released as the second single from the album and, like *Free To Fall* and *In Love With Love*, it came closest to achieving Top 40 status in the UK, where it charted at no.46. However, *Strike Me Pink* failed to chart anywhere else.

Platinum Pop

Platinum Pop is a medley of Blondie hits by This Year's Blonde, and featured *Hanging On The Telephone, Denis, Dreaming, Union City Blue, (I'm Always Touched by Your) Presence Dear, Picture This, Sunday Girl* and *Dreaming* (again). The single was issued in a small number of countries, including Germany, Italy and the UK, in 1981, and rose to no.46 in the UK during a five week chart run.

BLONDIE'S TOP 20 SINGLES

In this Top 20, each of Blondie and Deborah Harry's singles has been scored according to the following points system.

Points are given according to the peak position reached on the singles chart in each of the countries featured in this book:

    No.1:   100 points for the first week at no.1, plus 10 points for each additional week at no.1.

    No.2:   90 points for the first week at no.2, plus 5 points for each additional week at no.2.

No.3:	85 points.
No.4-6:	80 points.
No.7-10:	75 points.
No.11-15:	70 points.
No.16-20:	65 points.
No.21-30:	60 points.
No.31-40:	50 points.
No.41-50:	40 points.
No.51-60:	30 points.
No.61-70:	20 points.
No.71-80:	10 points.
No.81-100:	5 points.

Total weeks charted in each country are added, to give the final points score.

Reissues, remixes and re-entries of a single are counted together.

Rank/Single/Points

1. *Heart Of Glass* ~ 2524 points

2. *Call Me* ~ 1997 points

3. *The Tide Is High* ~ 1819 points

4. *Sunday Girl* ~ 1505 points

Rank/Single/Points

5   *Rapture* ~ 1350 points

6. *Maria* ~ 1204 points
7. *Dreaming* ~ 1153 points
8. *Atomic* ~ 1131 points
9. *Denis* ~ 1047 points
10. *French Kissin* ~ 696 points

11. *Island Of Lost Souls* ~ 668 points
12. *Hanging On The Telephone* ~ 412 points
13. *I Want That Man* ~ 406 points
14. *Backfired* ~ 369 points
15. *Union City Blue* ~ 311 points

16. *Rapture Riders* ~ 273 points
17. *New York, New York* ~ 272 points
18. *Picture This* ~ 236 points
19. *(I'm Always Touched By Your) Presence Dear* ~ 245 points
20. *One Way Or Another* ~ 160 points

Heart Of Glass is Blondie's most successful single globally by a comfortable margin, ahead of *Call Me* and The *Tide Is High*, with *Sunday Girl* and *Rapture* rounding off the Top 5.

As a solo artist, Deborah Harry's most successful single is *French Kissin*, which is ranks at no.10, two places but 251 points ahead of *I Want That Man*. Four singles credited to Deborah (one with Moby) feature in the Top 20, which is dominated by Blondie singles.

SINGLES TRIVIA

To date, Blondie has achieved 21 Top 40 singles in one or more of the countries featured in this book, with Debbie/Deborah solo adding a further eight Top 40 singles. There follows a country-by-country look at Blondie's and Deborah Harry's most successful hits.

Note: in the past, there was often one or more weeks over Christmas and New Year when no new chart was published in some countries. In such cases, the previous week's chart has been used to complete chart runs. Similarly, where a bi-weekly or monthly chart was in place, for chart runs these are counted as two and four weeks, respectively.

BLONDIE & DEBORAH HARRY IN AUSTRALIA

Most Hits

16 hits	Blondie
7 hits	Deborah Harry

Most Weeks

216 weeks	Blondie
91 weeks	Deborah Harry

No.1 Singles

1979   *Heart Of Glass/Sunday Girl*

Heart Of Glass/Sunday Girl topped the chart for 5 weeks.

Singles with the most weeks

27 weeks	*I Want That Man*
24 weeks	*In The Flesh*
24 weeks	*Heart Of Glass/Sunday Girl*
23 weeks	*Atomic*
21 weeks	*The Tide Is High*
21 weeks	*French Kissin In The USA*
20 weeks	*Call Me*
17 weeks	*Denis*
17 weeks	*Rush Rush*
16 weeks	*Rapture Riders*

BLONDIE IN AUSTRIA

Blondie achieved eight hit singles in Austria, which spent 106 weeks on the chart.

No.1 Singles

1979 *Heart Of Glass*

Heart Of Glass spent two months at no.1.

Singles with the most weeks

20 weeks	*Heart Of Glass*
16 weeks	*Denis*
16 weeks	*Maria*
14 weeks	*The Tide Is High*
12 weeks	*Sunday Girl*
12 weeks	*Atomic*
12 weeks	*Call Me*

BLONDIE & DEBORAH HARRY IN BELGIUM (Flanders)

Most Hits

15 hits	Blondie
3 hits	Deborah Harry

Most Weeks

127 weeks	Blondie
18 weeks	Deborah Harry

No.1 Singles

1978 *Denis*

Denis topped the chart for four weeks.

Singles with the most weeks

18 weeks	*Maria*
14 weeks	*Atomic*
11 weeks	*Denis*

11 weeks	*The Tide Is High*
10 weeks	*I'm Gonna Love You Too*
10 weeks	*Rapture Riders*
10 weeks	*French Kissin*
9 weeks	*Heart Of Glass*
9 weeks	*Rapture*
8 weeks	*(I'm Always Touched By Your) Presence Dear*
8 weeks	*Call Me*

BLONDIE IN CANADA

Between 1975 and 1996, Blondie achieved six hit singles in Canada, which spent 101 weeks on the chart.

No.1 Singles

1979	*Heart Of Glass*
1980	*Call Me*
1981	*The Tide Is High*
1981	*Rapture*

Most weeks at No.1

6 weeks	*Heart Of Glass*
6 weeks	*Call Me*
4 weeks	*The Tide Is High*
3 weeks	*Rapture*

Singles with the most weeks

28 weeks	*Heart Of Glass*
18 weeks	*Dreaming*
17 weeks	*Call Me*
16 weeks	*The Tide Is High*
12 weeks	*Rapture*

BLONDIE IN DENMARK

Blondie achieved five hits in Denmark, which spent 43 weeks on the chart.

The band's most successful single is *Sunday Girl*, which peaked at no.3.

Singles with the most weeks

18 weeks   *Heart Of Glass*
10 weeks   *The Tide Is High*
 9 weeks   *Sunday Girl*

BLONDIE IN FINLAND

Blondie achieved six hit singles in Finland, which spent 38 weeks on the chart.

The band's most successful single is *Call Me*, which peaked at no.3.

Singles with the most weeks

16 weeks   *Call Me*
 8 weeks   *Heart Of Glass*
 4 weeks   *Sunday Girl*
 4 weeks   *Dreaming*
 4 weeks   *The Tide Is High*

BLONDIE IN FRANCE

Blondie achieved 10 hit singles in France, which spent 199 weeks on the chart.

The band's most successful singles are *Heart Of Glass* and *Call Me*, which both peaked at no.4.

Singles with the most weeks

35 weeks   *Heart Of Glass*
35 weeks   *Atomic*
25 weeks   *Call Me*
19 weeks   *Sunday Girl*
18 weeks   *Island Of Lost Souls*
18 weeks   *Maria*
16 weeks   *The Tide Is High*
15 weeks   *Dreaming*
12 weeks   *Denis*

BLONDIE & DEBORAH HARRY IN GERMANY

Most Hits

13 hits   Blondie
2 hits   Deborah Harry

Most weeks

184 weeks   Blondie
14 weeks   Deborah Harry

No.1 Singles

1979   *Heart Of Glass*

Heart Of Glass topped the chart for 6 weeks.

Singles with the most weeks

28 weeks   *Heart Of Glass*
25 weeks   *Maria*
20 weeks   *Call Me*
19 weeks   *The Tide Is High*
18 weeks   *Sunday Girl*
15 weeks   *Denis*
14 weeks   *Atomic*
13 weeks   *Dreaming*
13 weeks   *Rapture*
10 weeks   *Union City Blue*
10 weeks   *French Kissin In The USA*

BLONDIE & DEBORAH HARRY IN IRELAND

Blondie achieved 14 hit singles in Ireland, which spent 97 weeks on the chart. Deborah Harry has achieved three hit singles, which spent 12 weeks on the chart.

No.1 Singles

1979   *Sunday Girl*

Sunday Girl topped the chart for 4 weeks.

Singles with the most weeks

11 weeks	*The Tide Is High*
10 weeks	*Heart Of Glass*
9 weeks	*Denis*
9 weeks	*Hanging On The Telephone*
9 weeks	*Sunday Girl*
9 weeks	*Maria*
8 weeks	*Dreaming*
6 weeks	*Call Me*
6 weeks	*Island Of Lost Souls*
6 weeks	*I Want That Man*

BLONDIE & DEBORAH HARRY IN ITALY

Blondie achieved five hit singles in Italy, which spent 47 weeks on the chart. Deborah Harry achieved one hit single, which spent just one week on the chart.

Blondie's highest charting single is *Heart Of Glass*, which peaked at no.8.

Singles with the most weeks

17 weeks	*Call Me*
19 weeks	*Heart Of Glass*
9 weeks	*Maria*

BLONDIE IN JAPAN

Blondie has achieved four hit singles in Japan, which spent 76 weeks on the chart.

Blondie's highest charting single is *Call Me*, which peaked at no.19.

Singles with the most weeks

39 weeks	*Call Me*
19 weeks	*Heart Of Glass*
10 weeks	*Sunday Girl*
8 weeks	*The Tide Is High*

BLONDIE & DEBORAH HARRY IN THE NETHERLANDS

Most Hits

14 hits   Blondie
3 hits   Deborah Harry

Most Weeks

120 weeks   Blondie
11 weeks   Deborah Harry

No.1 Singles

1978   *Denis*

Denis topped the chart for six weeks.

Singles with the most weeks

21 weeks   *Maria*
12 weeks   *Denis*
10 weeks   *I'm Gonna Love You Too*
10 weeks   *The Tide Is High*
9 weeks   *Heart Of Glass*
9 weeks   *Call Me*

BLONDIE & DEBORAH HARRY IN NEW ZEALAND

Most Hits

12 hits   Blondie
4 hits   Deborah Harry

Most Weeks

117 weeks   Blondie
30 weeks   Deborah Harry

No.1 Singles

1979   *Heart Of Glass*
1981   *The Tide Is High*

Most weeks at no.1

4 weeks	*Heart Of Glass*
2 weeks	*The Tide Is High*

Singles with the most weeks

24 weeks	*Heart Of Glass*
16 weeks	*Atomic*
15 weeks	*Dreaming*
14 weeks	*The Tide Is High*
12 weeks	*Call Me*
12 weeks	*French Kissin In The USA*
12 weeks	*I Want That Man*
10 weeks	*Island Of Lost Souls*
10 weeks	*Maria*
8 weeks	*Rapture*

BLONDIE IN NORWAY

Blondie achieved seven hit singles in Norway, which spent 59 weeks on the chart.

The band's most successful single is *Call Me*, which peaked at no.2.

Singles with the most weeks

15 weeks	*Call Me*
13 weeks	*Sunday Girl*
8 weeks	*Heart Of Glass*
8 weeks	*Dreaming*
8 weeks	*Atomic*

BLONDIE IN SOUTH AFRICA

Blondie achieved six hit singles in South Africa, which spent 64 weeks on the chart.

The band's most successful singles are *Heart Of Glass* and *Call Me*, which both peaked at no.2.

Singles with the most weeks

17 weeks	*Heart Of Glass*
15 weeks	*Call Me*

12 weeks	*The Tide Is High*
8 weeks	*Rapture*
7 weeks	*Sunday Girl*

BLONDIE IN SPAIN

Blondie achieved four hit singles in Spain, which spent 38 weeks on the chart.

No.1 Singles

1999	*Maria*

Maria spent a solitary week at no.1.

Singles with the most weeks

16 weeks	*Heart Of Glass*
14 weeks	*Maria*
5 weeks	*Rapture*

BLONDIE & DEBORAH HARRY IN SWEDEN

Most Hits

9 hits	Blondie
1 hit	Deborah Harry

Most Weeks

82 weeks	Blondie
2 weeks	Deborah Harry

Blondie's most successful singles in Sweden are *Heart Of Glass* and *Call Me*, which both peaked at no.3.

Singles with the most weeks

24 weeks	*Heart Of Glass*
24 weeks	*Maria*
20 weeks	*Call Me*
4 weeks	*Rapture*

BLONDIE & DEBORAH HARRY IN SWITZERLAND

Most Hits

5 hits   Blondie
1 hit   Deborah Harry

Most Weeks

76 weeks   Blondie
2 weeks   Deborah Harry

No.1 Singles

1979   *Heart Of Glass*

Heart Of Glass topped the chart for three weeks.

Singles with the most weeks

27 weeks   *Maria*
15 weeks   *Call Me*
14 weeks   *Heart Of Glass*
10 weeks   *Sunday Girl*
10 weeks   *The Tide Is High*

BLONDIE & DEBORAH HARRY IN THE UNITED KINGDOM

Most Hits

18 hits   Blondie
13 hits   Deborah Harry

Most weeks

196 weeks   Blondie
62 weeks   Deborah Harry

No.1 Singles

1979   *Heart Of Glass*
1979   *Sunday Girl*
1980   *Atomic*

1980 *Call Me*
1980 *The Tide Is High*
1999 *Maria*

Most weeks at No.1

4 weeks *Heart Of Glass*
3 weeks *Sunday Girl*
2 weeks *Atomic*
2 weeks *The Tide Is High*

Singles with the most weeks

17 weeks *Denis*
17 weeks *Maria*
16 weeks *Heart Of Glass*
14 weeks *Atomic*
13 weeks *Sunday Girl*
13 weeks *Call Me*
12 weeks *Hanging On The Telephone*
12 weeks *Union City Blue*
12 weeks *The Tide Is High*
11 weeks *Picture This*

The BRIT Certified/BPI (British Phonographic Industry) Awards

The BPI began certifying Silver, Gold & Platinum singles in 1973. From 1973 to 1988: Silver = 250,000, Gold = 500,000 & Platinum = 1 million. From 1989 onwards: Silver = 200,000, Gold = 400,000 & Platinum = 600,000. Awards are based on shipments, not sales; however, in July 2013 the BPI automated awards, based on actual sales (including streaming) since February 1994.

Platinum *Heart Of Glass* (February 1979) = 1 million
Platinum *Maria* (February 2021) = 600,000
Gold *Denis* (March 1978) = 500,000
Gold *Sunday Girl* (June 1979) = 500,000
Gold *Atomic* (March 1980) = 500,000
Gold *The Tide Is High* (November 1980) = 500,000
Gold *Call Me* (July 2021) = 500,000
Gold *One Way Or Another* (January 2022) = 400,000
Silver *Picture This* (September 1978) = 250,000
Silver *Hanging On The Telephone* (December 1978) = 250,000
Silver *Dreaming* (September 1979) = 250,000

Silver   *Union City Blue* (December 1979) = 250,000
Silver   *Rapture* (January 1981) = 250,000

BLONDIE & DEBORAH HARRY IN THE UNITED STATES

Most Hits

10 hits   Blondie
 4 hits   Deborah Harry

Most weeks

148 weeks   Blondie
 31 weeks   Deborah Harry

No.1 Singles

1979   *Heart Of Glass*
1980   *Call Me*
1981   *The Tide Is High*
1981   *Rapture*

Most weeks at No.1

6 weeks   *Call Me*
2 weeks   *Rapture*

Singles with the most weeks

26 weeks   *The Tide Is High*
25 weeks   *Call Me*
21 weeks   *Heart Of Glass*
20 weeks   *Rapture*
14 weeks   *One Way Or Another*
14 weeks   *Dreaming*
11 weeks   *French Kissin In The USA*
10 weeks   *Island Of Lost Souls*
10 weeks   *Backfired*
 9 weeks   *Atomic*

RIAA (Recording Industry Association of America) Awards

The RIAA began certifying Gold singles in 1958 and Platinum singles in 1976. From 1958 to 1988: Gold = 1 million, Platinum = 2 million. From 1988 onwards: Gold = 500,000, Platinum = 1 million. Awards are based on shipments, not sales.

Gold	*Heart Of Glass* (April 1979)	= 1 million
Gold	*Call Me* (April 1980)	= 1 million
Gold	*The Tide Is High* (January 1981)	= 1 million
Gold	*Rapture* (March 1981)	= 1 million

BLONDIE IN ZIMBABWE

Blondie achieved eight hit singles in Zimbabwe, which spent 72 weeks on the chart.

No.1 Singles

1979   *Heart Of Glass*

Heart Of Glass spent just one week at no.1.

Singles with the most weeks

16 weeks	*Heart Of Glass*
14 weeks	*Sunday Girl*
13 weeks	*Call Me*
11 weeks	*The Tide Is High*
7 weeks	*Denis*

All The Top 40 Albums

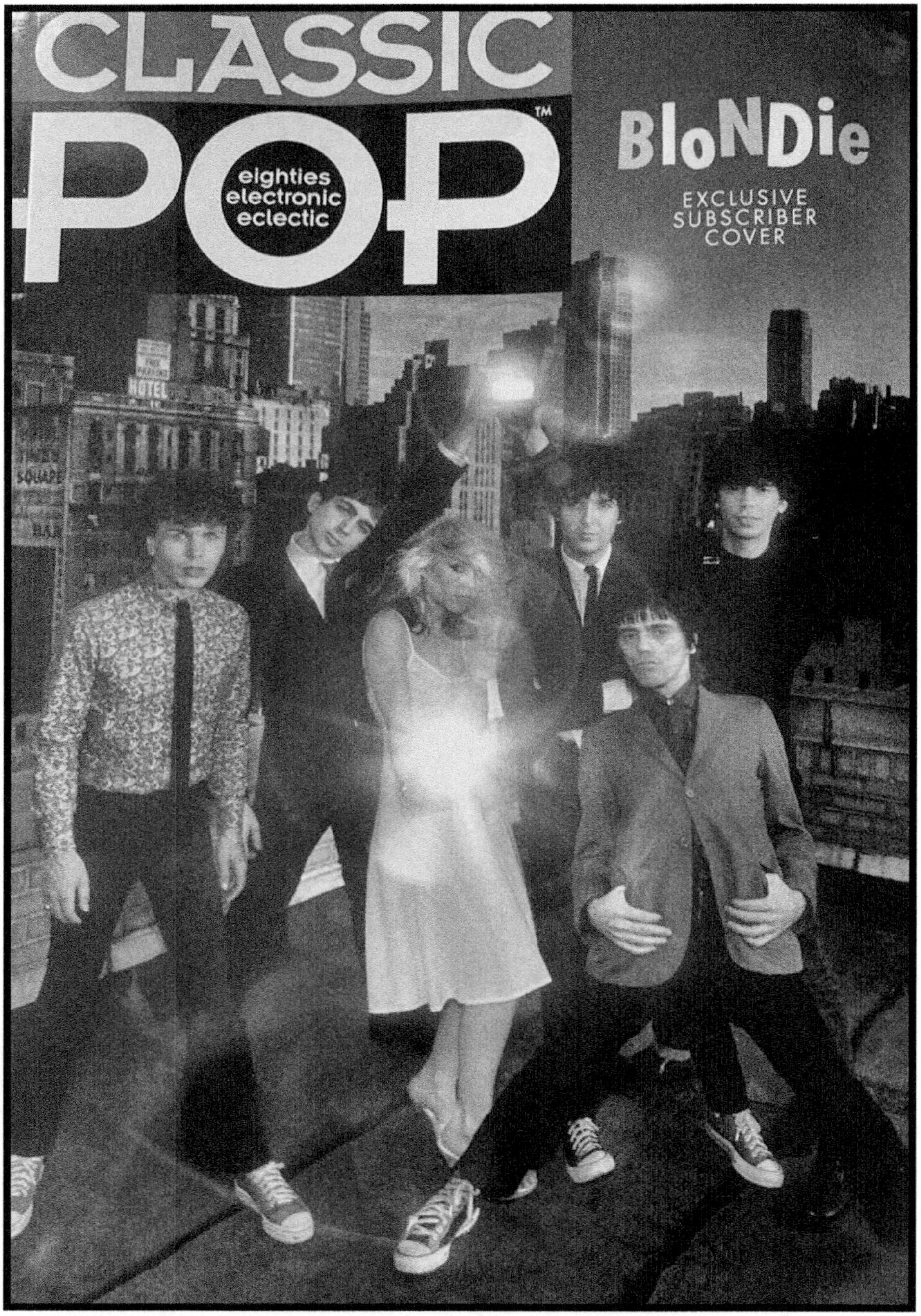
CLASSIC
POP
eighties
electronic
eclectic
BloNDie
EXCLUSIVE
SUBSCRIBER
COVER
HOTEL

1 ~ BLONDIE

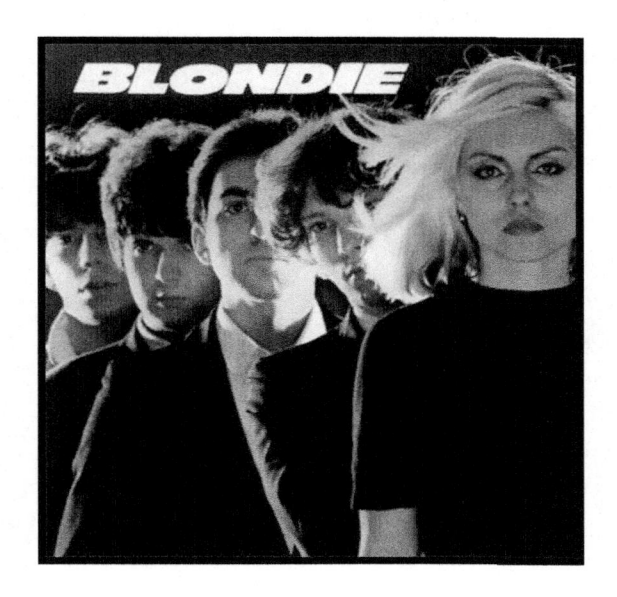

X Offender/Little Girl Lies/In The Flesh/Look Good In Blue/In The Sun/A Shark In Jets Clothing/Man Overboard/Rip Her To Shreds/Rifle Range/Kung Fu Girls/The Attack Of The Giant Ants

Produced by Richard Gottehrer & Craig Leon.

USA: Private Stock Records PS 2023 (1976).

BLONDIE wasn't a hit in the United States.

UK: Private Stock Records PVLP 1017 (1977).

10.03.79: **75**

Australia
5.09.77: peaked at no.**14**, charted for 24 weeks

Blondie recorded their debut, self-titled album in August and September 1976 at New York City's Plaza Sound Studios. The album was originally released in December of the same year by Private Stock Records, but it wasn't a hit anywhere. A single, *X Offender*, was originally titled *Sex Offender*, but the title was changed as radio was unlikely to play a single so titled. The single, like the album, wasn't a hit anywhere.

Unhappy with the lack of sales and promotion, Blondie bought out their contract with Private Stock Records, and signed with Chrysalis in 1977. *BLONDIE* was reissued in September 1977, along with a new single, *In The Flesh*, which rose to no.2 in Australia. The success of the single led to the album charting for the first time as well, and it achieved no.14 in Australia. However, both the single and album didn't do much anywhere else, although as Blondie's popularity grew, so the band's debut album belatedly charted at no.75 in the UK.

Three singles were released from *BLONDIE*: *X Offender*, *In The Flesh* and *Rip Her To Shreds*. Of these, only *In The Flesh* achieved Top 40 status anywhere.

BLONDIE was remastered and reissued in 2001, with five bonus tracks:

- *Out In The Streets (Original Instant Records Demo)*
- *The Thin Line (Original Instant Records Demo)*
- *Platinum Blonde (Original Instant Records Demo)*
- *X Offender (Original Private Stock Single Version)*
- *In The Sun (Original Private Stock Single Version)*

2 ~ PLASTIC LETTERS

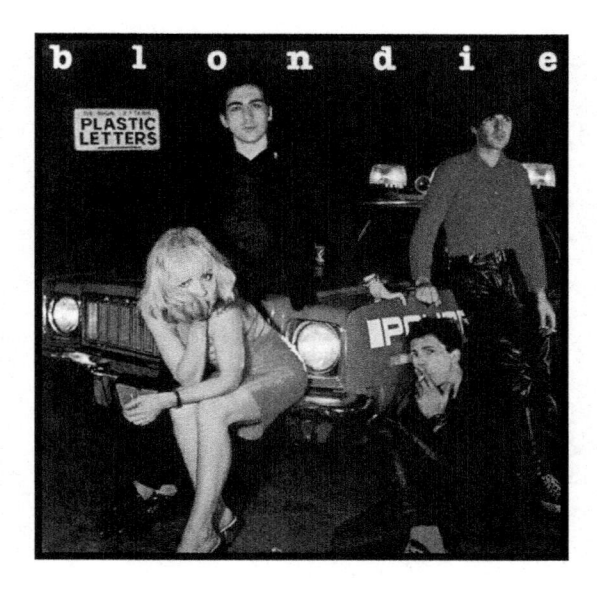

Fan Mail/Denis/Bermuda Triangle Blues (Flight 45)/Youth Nabbed As Sniper/Contact In Red Square/(I'm Always Touched By Your) Presence Dear/I'm On E/I Didn't Have The Nerve To Say No/Love At The Pier/No Imagination/Kidnapper/Detroit 442/Cautious Lip

Produced by Richard Gottehrer.

USA: Chrysalis CHR 1166 (1978).

25.03.78: 98-87-77-**72**

UK: Chrysalis CHR 1166 (1978).

4.03.78: 40-21-12-12-**10**-14-14-12-20-22-25-27-27-18-20-24-29-48-44-53-x-57
20.01.79: 68-60-x-39-35-29-30-31-30-49-43-45-41-53-58-38-60-68-x-52-69-46-45-53-66-
   59-59-64-71-56-66-71-57-58-62

Australia
6.03.78: peaked at no.**64**, charted for 15 weeks

Netherlands
25.02.78: 9-5-3-3-**2**-3-3-6-6-12-12-14-16-24-24-25-20-35-33-42-48

New Zealand
27.05.79: 48-45-**38**-46

YOU DON'T HAVE TO BE A VINYL JUNKIE TO GET A BLAST FROM 'PLASTIC LETTERS.'

Sweden
10.03.78: **33** (bi-weekly)
5.05.78: 40-42-44 (bi-weekly)

Blondie's second album, *PLASTIC LETTERS*, was recorded in June and July 1977 but wasn't released until the following February. Like the band's eponymous debut, it was recorded at Plaza Sound Studio, New York City, and produced by Richard Gottehrer.

The album produced two hit singles:

- *Denis*
- *(I'm Always Touched By Your) Presence Dear*

A third track, *Kidnapper*, was issued as a single in Japan only but it wasn't a hit.

PLASTIC LETTERS sold better than *BLONDIE*, and charted at no.2 in the Netherlands, no.10 in the UK, no.33 in Sweden and no.38 in New Zealand. However, it was only a minor hit in Australia and the USA.

PLASTIC LETTERS has been remastered and reissued twice. In 1994, the album was reissued with two bonus tracks:

- *Poet's Problem*
- *Denis (Alternative Version)*

Poet's Problem was the B-side of *(I'm Always Touched By Your) Presence Dear*.

In 2001, *PLASTIC LETTERS* was reissued again, this time with four bonus tracks:

- *Once I Had A Love* (aka *The Disco Song*)
- *Scenery*

- *Poet's Problem*
- *Detroit 442 (Live)*

The Disco Song is an early version of Blondie's most successful single, *Heart Of Glass*. *Scenery* is an outtake from the *BLONDIE album*. The live version of *Detroit 442* was recorded at the Walnut Theatre, Philadelphia, in November 1978.

3 ~ PARALLEL LINES

Hanging On The Telephone/One Way Or Another/Picture This/Fade Away And Radiate/ Pretty Baby/I Know But I Don't Know/11:59/Will Anything Happen/Sunday Girl/Heart Of Glass/I'm Gonna Love You Too/Just Go Away

Produced by Mike Chapman.

USA: Chrysalis CHR 1192 (1978).

20.10.78: 96-91-87-85-85-90-94
10.02.79: 97-95-82-72-53-40-30-25-21-13-8-**6-6-6**-9-12-13-14-21-34-34-44-44-46-46-48-
   47-46-57-56-65-65-75-83-100
15.03.80: 86-84-81-84-86-90-93-92-91-97-97-97-99-96-96

UK: Chrysalis CHR 1192 (1978).

23.09.78: 13-9-7-11-16-14-18-22-26-30-28-21-21-16-16-16-16-9-3-4-3-**1-1-1-1**-2-2-3-6-8-7-8-
   9-10-11-9-6-3-5-3-3-2-4-5-4-5-5-10-10-8-8-8-8-15-13-18-11-12-16-14-21-25-30-31-29-38-
   27-27-28-15-15-18-17-22-26-35-30-32-26-31-43-41-41-36-53-60-53-56-62-63-54-72-56-52-
   62-74-x-x-61-30-68-46-49-66-73-60-71
12.04.03: 77-72-90
10.04.04: 60-63-79
10.07.04: 84-76
6.10.07: 88

Australia
13.11.78: peaked at no.**2**, charted for 33 weeks

Austria
15.07.79: **24** (monthly)

Blondes ARE more fun

BLONDIE: 'Plastic Letters' (Chrysalis Chr 1166)

FOR THE first time I can take Blondie seriously (but with a hidden smile).

That debut album had spirit, and sass, and a nice picture on the front. But the music was scraps, bits of this era, bits of that.

'Plastic Letters' is plastic music, shiny and Dayglo, no ugly fault lines. No more Debbie Harry's voice squeaking apologetically, now the vocal is actually sensuous, beefed up and filed down to needle point, jab jab, hurts good.

'Plastic Letters' is more musical, more freaky. It's what every second album must have, every groove has to announce progression.

Blondie are still a pop band, but a very unusual one, plastic out of no mould. Blondie's songs aren't hummable, just commercial, and instant.

Debbie Harry is neither of the things her accusers suggest ie a glamour girl who eclipses Blondie as a band or a talentless visual gimmick sold like cornflakes. The band on this album are vital fun, no musical mekanoids, smart as suits and with a direction they never suggested on the first album.

And Debbie has other talents outside big eyes and angel's cheekbones. Her voice, though never classically brilliant, now finds corners it never found before, coils round the sound wall like a real pop queen, no false idol.

The first album claimed it, 'Plastic Letters' proves it. Blondes really are more fun. + + + +
TIM LOTT

Finland
10.78: peaked at no.**11**, charted for 30 weeks

Germany
26.03.79: 14-**9**-11-**9**-12-10-12-14-13-11-14-11-11-11-14-12-15-16-19-15-27-23-24-20-31-33-37-44-45-x-42

Italy
12.05.79: peaked at no.**13**, charted for 15 weeks

Japan
20.11.78: peaked at no.**56**, charted for 12 weeks

Netherlands
16.09.78: 17-**7**-9-11-10-18-20-33-33-42-43-36-32-30

New Zealand
26.11.78: 29-29
25.02.79: 22-19-18-18-16-8-8-**3**-4-4-**3**-4-4-**3**-4-6-7-10-15-19-19-20-24-31-28-19-21-22-26-30-30-30-35-31-42-42-49-30-47

Parallel Lines go round in circles.

Blondie's latest album is out now. Called 'Parallel Lines,' it's their third, and their finest album to date.

12 pulsating tracks, including their current smash single 'Picture This.'

Don't miss 'Parallel Lines.' Circulate your record shop. Now.

BLONDIE: PARALLEL LINES CDL 1192
also available on cassette.

TOUR DATES & VENUES

Sat.	9 Sept.	Hammersmith	Odeon
Sun.	10 Sept.	Portsmouth	Guildhall
Tues.	12 Sept.	Newcastle	City Hall
Wed.	13 Sept.	Edinburgh	Odeon
Thur.	14 Sept.	Manchester	Free Trade Hall
Fri.	15 Sept.	Birmingham	Odeon
Sat.	16 Sept.	Hammersmith	Odeon

ALL SHOWS SOLD OUT EXCEPT THE EXTRA 4 pm SHOW WHICH HAS BEEN ADDED DUE TO PUBLIC DEMAND HAMMERSMITH ODEON SATURDAY SEPTEMBER 16th.

SUPPORT ACT: THE BOYFRIENDS

Chrysalis

Norway
21.10.78: **16**-17-18
24.03.79: 19-19
24.11.79: 38

Spain
4.06.79: peaked at no.**24**, charted for 9 weeks

Sweden
6.10.78: 15-**9-9**-16-15-20-26-26-25-25-33-41-31-29-28-31-21-34-25-30-29-43-49-36-41-40-40-44 (bi-weekly)

Zimbabwe
4.08.79: peaked at no.**12**

Blondie's third album was recorded at New York City's Record Plant studio with Australian producer, Mike Chapman, whom the band had met whilst on tour in California. Peter Leeds, the band's manager, and Chrysalis Records were instrumental in encouraging Blondie and Chapman to work together, but Chapman has admitted he found Blondie difficult to work with, and remembers them as the worst band he had ever worked with in terms of musical ability.

'The Blondies were tough in the studio, real tough,' he said. 'None of them liked each other, except Chris and Debbie, and there was so much animosity. They were really, really juvenile in their approach to life, a classic New York underground rock band, and they didn't give a f**k about anything.'

Debbie admitted, 'We weren't prepared for his (Mike Chapman's) level of expertise so we learned an enormous amount about how to record from him. His approach was very different to (Richard) Gottehrer's. Chapman helped us become more commercial, with tighter arrangements and perfect basic tracks.'

Chrysalis gave Blondie and Chapman six months to complete the band's third album, but they did so in just six weeks, in June and July 1977. Released two months later, the album was titled after an unfinished Debbie Harry track that didn't make the album's final cut. The photographs of the band used on the sleeve was chosen by Blondie's manager, which Debbie and Chris were both unhappy about; the male members of the band were all smiling, but Debbie looked icy. Both had been asked to select images of themselves, for the cover, and weren't happy that images they'd rejected were used instead.

PARALLEL LINES went on to become Blondie's most successful album, producing six hit singles:

- *Picture This*
- *I'm Gonna Love You Too*
- *Hanging On The Telephone*
- *Heart Of Glass*

- *Sunday Girl*
- *One Way Or Another*

The album gave Blondie their first no.1 album in the UK, where it topped the chart for four straight weeks. Elsewhere, the album charted at no.2 in Australia, no.3 in New Zealand, no.6 in the United States, no.7 in the Netherlands, no.9 in Germany and Sweden, no.11 in Finland, no.12 in Zimbabwe, no.13 in Italy, no.16 in Norway, and no.24 in Austria and Spain.

From 1979 onwards, all pressings of *PARALLEL LINES* saw the original album version of *Heart Of Glass* replaced with the disco version.

PARALLEL LINES was remastered and reissued in 2001, with four bonus tracks:

- *Once I Had A Love (aka The Disco Song) (1978 Version)*
- *Bang A Gong (Get It On) (Live*
- *I Know But I Don't Know (Live)*
- *Hanging On The Telephone (Live)*

Blondie's live cover of T. Rex's *Get It On* was recorded at The Paradise, Boston, in 1978. *I Know But I Don't Know* was also recorded in November 1978, but at the Walnut Theatre, Philadelphia. The live version of *Hanging On The Telephone* was recorded in Dallas in 1980.

Deluxe Collectors Edition

A Deluxe Collectors Edition of *PARALLEL LINES* was released in 2008. It came with a new sleeve design, four bonus tracks and a bonus DVD.

The bonus tracks were:

- *Heart Of Glass (7" Single Version)*
- *Sunday Girl (French Version)*

- *Hanging On The Telephone (Nosebleed Handbag Remix)*
- *Fade Away And Radiate (108 BPM Remix)*

The bonus DVD featured the music videos for *Heart Of Glass*, *Hanging On The Telephone* and *Picture This*, plus Blondie's live performance of *Sunday Girl* on *Top Of The Tops*.

The Mail On Sunday, a British newspaper, gave away copies of *PARALLEL LINES* in a card sleeve in 2010, with two bonus tracks: *What I Heard* and *Girlie Girlie*. Both tracks subsequently featured on Blondie's 2011 album, *PANIC OF GIRLS*.

4 ~ EAT TO THE BEAT

Dreaming/The Hardest Part/Union City Blue/Shayla/Eat To The Beat/Accidents Never Happen/ Die Young Stay Pretty/Slow Motion/Atomic/Sound-A-Sleep/Victor/Living In The Real World

Produced by Mike Chapman.

USA: Chrysalis CDL 1225 (1979).

20.10.79: 51-30-27-26-19-**17-17-17**-24-33-33-51-49-48-42-40-45-41-34-33-32-30-29-32-
36-39-43-55-55-55-53-51-49-58-58-58-66-69-97-97-95-95

UK: Chrysalis CDL 1225 (1979).

12.10.79: **1**-2-2-3-3-12-17-21-20-14-17-17-17-15-7-14-21-21-32-31-33-17-14-11-16-19-
25-27-30-39-32-44-34-38-45-65-64-71

Australia
1.10.79: peaked at no.**9**, charted for 52 weeks

Austria
15.11.79: **19** (monthly)

Finland
10.79: peaked at no.**3**, charted for 18 weeks

Blondie
THE NEW ALBUM
EAT TO THE BEAT
includes the single
DREAMING
Produced by MIKE CHAPMAN
L.P. CDL 1225

Germany
29.10.79: **23**-32-29-38-38
14.01.80: 56-x-64-x-63

Japan
20.10.79: peaked at no.**27**, charted for 8 weeks

Netherlands
20.10.79: 37-**16**-22-23-35-36

New Zealand
18.11.79: **3**-6-7-13-17-21-21-21-21-24-29-29-35-34-43-38-37-45-43-43-x-x-40-45-31-24-25-26-48-27-29-35-36-39-44

Norway
20.10.79: 9-7-**6**-9-11-11-17-26-36-36-34-34-34-22-15-10-8-8-**6**-8-10-11-13-15-19-19-18

Sweden
5.10.79: 21-3-**2**-4-6-15-18-33-45-50 (bi-weekly)

Blondie recorded their fourth studio album in May and June 1979, at two New York City studios, Electric Lady Studios and The Power Station. Once again, the album was produced by Mike Chapman.

Unusually, as well as an album, the band shot music videos to all twelve tracks on *EAT TO THE BEAT*, and released them as a video album. Eleven of the promos were filmed in New York but the twelfth, *Union City Blue*, was filmed at Union Dry Dock in Weehawken, New Jersey.

The album generated four hit singles:

- *Dreaming*
- *Union City Blue*
- *The Hardest Part*
- *Atomic*

The release of a fifth track, *Slow Motion*, as the follow-up to *Atomic* was shelved, following the success of *Call Me*, which Blondie recorded as the theme song to the 1980 movie, *American Gigolo*.

EAT TO THE BEAT gave Blondie their second no.1 album in the UK, and elsewhere it achieved no.2 in Sweden, no.3 in Finland and New Zealand, no.6 in Norway, no.9 in Australia, no.16 in the Netherlands, no.17 in the United States, no.19 in Austria, no.23 in Germany and no.27 in Japan.

144

EAT TO THE BEAT was remastered and reissued in 2001, with four bonus tracks:

- *Die Young Stay Pretty (Live)*
- *Seven Rooms Of Gloom (Live)*
- *Heroes (Live)*
- *Ring Of Fire (Live)*

Die Young Stay Pretty and *Seven Rooms Of Gloom* were recorded on New Year's Eve 1979 at the Apollo Theatre in Glasgow, Scotland. Blondie's cover of David Bowie's *Heroes*, which also served as the B-side to *Atomic*, was recorded at London's Hammersmith Odeon on 12th January 1980. The cover of the Johnny Cash hit, *Ring Of Fire*, was Blondie's contribution to the soundtrack album for the 1980 film, *ROADIE*.

In his liner notes for the 2001 reissue, producer Mike Chapman revealed during the recording of *EAT TO THE BEAT* drugs 'found their way into the studio and presented us with yet another obstacle. The more drugs, the more fights. It was becoming a real mess ... the music was good but the group was showing signs of wear and tear.'

The remastered version of *EAT TO THE BEAT* was reissued again in 2007, minus the four bonus track included on the 2001 release, but with a bonus DVD of the long deleted video album.

BRAVO

SEXY-GIRL BLONDIE
Autogrammkarte
mit allen Daten

3 POSTERS

CLOUT

MILK & HONEY

DSCHINGIS KHAN

Heiße Bilder:
LIZ Die schönste Frau der Welt

Mit den **TEENS** auf Tour

Neue Foto-Love-Story

AUFKLÄRUNG: WAS DEIN PARTNER EMPFINDET

5 ~ AUTOAMERICAN

Europa/Live It Up/Here's Looking At You/The Tide Is High/Angels On The Balcony/Go Through It/Do The Dark/Rapture/Faces/T-Birds/Walk Like Me/Follow Me

Cassette bonus track: *Susie And Jeffrey*.

Produced by Mike Chapman.

USA: Chrysalis CHE 1290 (1980).

13.12.80: 20-18-15-15-13-11-10-10-9-8-**7-7-7-7-7**-12-12-12-13-12-17-25-29-47-69-73-83-88

UK: Chrysalis CDL 1290 (1980).

29.11.80: **3**-4-7-13-12-12-14-17-27-27-24-25-21-33-45-53

Australia
8.12.80: peaked at no.**8**, charted for 30 weeks

Austria
1.01.81: 20-**18**-20 (bi-weekly)

Finland
11.80: peaked at no.**16**, charted for 12 weeks

147

Virgin
UP TO £2 OFF VIRGIN TOP 60 ALBUMS WEEKLY
BLONDIE 'AUTOAMERICAN' THE NEW ALBUM- AUTOMATICALLY AT VIRGIN FOR JUST £3-99.
JUST A FEW OF THIS WEEK'S SPECIAL ALBUM OFFERS AT VIRGIN...
STEELY DAN
JOHN LENNON
PUBLIC IMAGE
BAUHAUS
THE MODETTES
BLACK SABBATH
BAD MANNERS
BILLY JOEL
GEORGE BENSON
THE SEX PISTOLS
TANGERINE DREAM
POLICE
NEIL YOUNG
THE DAMNED
DEEP PURPLE
ALBUM OR CASSETTE ONLY £3·99
THE VIRGIN MEGASTORES
14 Oxford Street, London W.1. (Near Tottenham Court Road) Tel: 01-631 1234
28/32 Union Street, Glasgow Telephone: 041-221 0103

Germany
29.12.80: 63-58-61-55-57-57-**42**-60-63-63

Italy
14.02.81: peaked at no.**17**, charted for 2 weeks

Japan
1.12.80: peaked at no.**20**, charted for 15 weeks

Netherlands
13.12.80: **16**-18-38-38-50

New Zealand
18.01.81: 22-12-9-**6-6**-7-9-9-13-17-19-17-18-16-22-25-31-33-49-x-43

Norway
29.11.80: 29-22-22-13-25-25-25-25-**12**-16-19-25-37-37

Sweden
28.11.80: 13-**11**-16-15-19-29-30 (bi-weekly)

Blondie's fifth studio album, at the insistence of producer Mike Chapman, was recorded at Hollywood's United Western Recorders studio. However, the band was equally insistent the cover art be shot in their home town, and it features a photograph of the band atop the roof of New York's 300 Mercer Street.
    Only two singles were lifted from *AUTOAMERICAN*, but both became global hits:

- *The Tide Is High*
- *Rapture*

The B-side of *The Tide Is High*, *Susie (*aka *Suzy) & Jeffrey*, was only included on the cassette release of *AUTOAMERICAN*.
    AUTOAMERICAN broke Blondie's run of no.1 albums in the UK, where it made its chart debut at no.3, but climbed no higher. Elsewhere, the album achieved no.6 in New Zealand, no.7 in the United States, no.8 in Australia, no.11 in Sweden, no.12 in Norway, no.16 in Finland and the Netherlands, no.17 in Italy, no.18 in Austria, no.20 in Japan and no.42 in Germany.
    AUTOAMERICAN was remastered and reissued in 1994, with two bonus tracks:

- *Rapture (Special Disco Mix)*
- *Live It Up (Special Disco Mix)*

AUTOAMERICAN was remastered and reissued a second time in 2001, this time with three bonus tracks:

- *Call Me (Original Long Version)*
- *Suzy & Jeffrey*
- *Rapture (Special Disco Mix)*

6 ~ KOOKOO

Jump Jump/The Jam Was Moving/Chrome/Surrender/Inner City Spillover/Backfired/Now I Know You Know/Under Arrest/Military Rap/Oasis

Produced by Nile Rogers & Bernard Edwards.

USA: Chrysalis CHR 1347 (1981).

29.08.81: 51-31-28-26-**25**-42-57-57-59-74

UK: Chrysalis CHR 1347 (1981).

8.08.81: 9-**6**-12-21-24-44-66

Australia
21.09.81: peaked at no.**16**, charted for 11 weeks

Japan
1.09.81: peaked at no.**35**, charted for 11 weeks

Sweden
14.08.81: 10-**7**-14-30-46 (bi-weekly)

Debbie Harry recorded her first solo album *KOOKOO* while she and boyfriend Chris Stein were taking a break from Blondie.

Debbie and Chris wrote four songs for the album, as did producers Bernard Edwards and Nile Rodgers, who Blondie had met while recording *EAT TO THE BEAT* in New York in 1979. The remaining two songs, *Under Arrest* and *Oasis*, were composed by Debbie and Chris with Bernard and Nile.

The album's distinctive sleeve was designed by Swiss artist H.R. Giger, who had won an Oscar for the popular 1979 film, *Alien.*

'I remember she wanted to change the name from Blondie to Deborah Harry,' said Giger, 'so the first thing was to change her hair colour.'

Giger asked Debbie for a portrait of herself, and she sent him a headshot by the British photographer, Brian Aris.

'At the time,' said Giger, 'a friend of mine was a doctor who made acupuncture where they went into your ear with little needles. I was very impressed by this, so I took very big needles and I used them for her portrait. I stuck them through her picture, then I airbrushed it so it looked like the needles went through her head to suggest stimulation, to turn on the four elements: Earth, Air, Fire, Water.'

Debbie was very happy with the result, not least because it was such a departure from Blondie, but the image proved controversial.

Officials from London Underground deemed the images of Debbie with large metal needles piercing her face and neck too disturbing, and refused to permit promotional posters for the album to be displayed in any London Underground stations.

Two singles were released from the album in most countries, and both achieved Top 40 status:

- *Backfired*
- *The Jam Was Moving*

Chrome was also issued as a single in select European countries, including Germany, while *Jump Jump* was released as a single in Peru ~ neither single was a hit.

KOOKOO charted at no.6 in the UK, no.7 in Sweden, no.16 in Australia, no.25 in the United States and no.35 in Japan.

KOOKOO was remastered and reissued on CD in 1994 with two bonus tracks:

- *Backfired (12" Mix)*
- *The Jam Was Moving (12" Mix)*

Five years later, *KOOKOO* was reissued on CD in the United States with one bonus track, *Backfired (12" Mix)*.

30th Anniversary Edition

In 2011, to mark the album's 30th anniversary, *KOOKOO* was reissued on CD with three bonus tracks:

- *Backfired (12" Mix)*
- *The Jam Was Moving (12" Mix)*
- *Inner City Spillover (12" Mix)*

7 ~ THE BEST OF BLONDIE / BLONDIE'S HITS

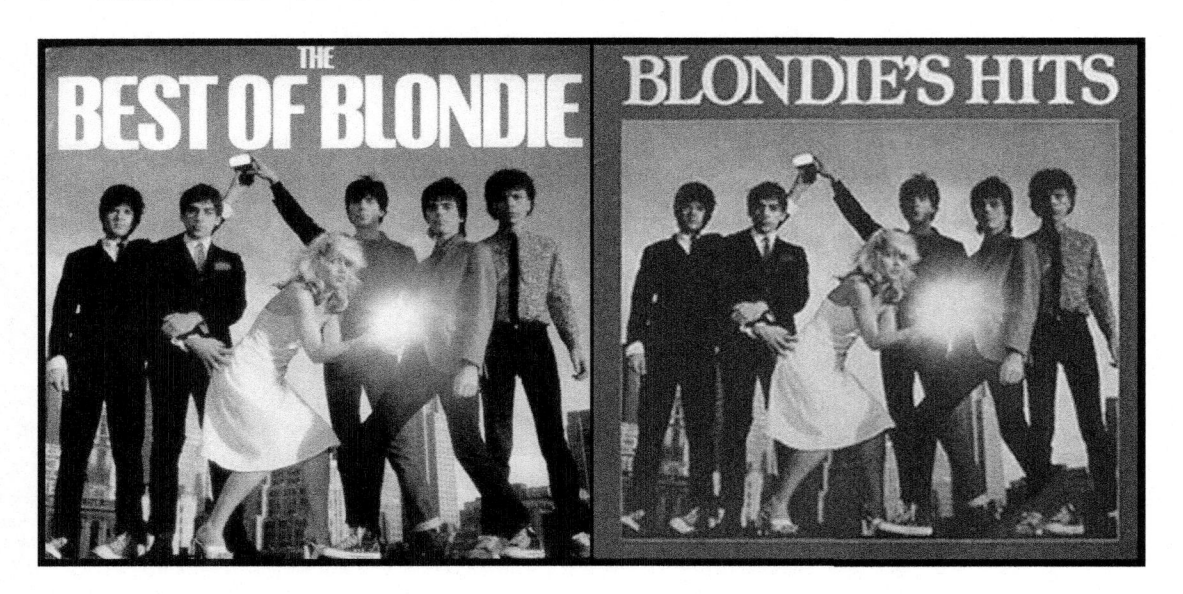

USA: *Heart Of Glass (Remix)/Dreaming/The Tide Is High/In The Flesh (Remix)/Sunday Girl (Remix)/Hanging On The Telephone/Rapture (Remix)/One Way Or Another/(I'm Always Touched By Your) Presence Dear/Call Me/Atomic/Rip Her To Shreds*

UK: *Heart Of Glass (Remix)/Denis/The Tide Is High/In The Flesh (Remix)/Sunday Girl (Remix)/Dreaming/Hanging On The Telephone/Rapture (Remix)/Picture This/(I'm Always Touched By Your) Presence Dear/ Call Me/Atomic/Rip Her To Shreds*

USA: Chrysalis CHR 1337 (1981).

31.10.81: 78-58-45-35-32-32-**30-30**-38-38-38-38-35-36-58-67-74-84

UK: Chrysalis CDL TV1 (1981).

31.10.81: **4**-5-7-6-5-7-7-8-9-9-12-21-23-26-39-50-58-60-67-66-62-74-92
24.08.85: 94-54-96-83-x-x-87
19.04.86: 88
17.01.87: 96-79-80-x-x-x-91-x-94-86-100-93-x-x-x-97
5.03.88: 84-99

Australia
21.12.81: peaked at no.**1** (2), charted for 23 weeks

Japan
21.10.81: peaked at no.**34**, charted for 9 weeks

THE
BEST OF BLONDIE
14 GREAT TRACKS
HEART OF GLASS • DENIS • THE TIDE IS HIGH • CALL ME
SUNDAY GIRL • RAPTURE • ATOMIC • HANGING ON THE TELEPHONE
DREAMING • PRESENCE DEAR • PICTURE THIS • UNION CITY BLUE • IN THE FLESH • RIP HER TO SHREDS
ALBUM INCLUDES
FULL COLOUR POSTER

Netherlands
14.11.81: 49-x-**46**

New Zealand
20.12.81: 23-**1-1-1**-2-4-9-13-13-17-43-47

Zimbabwe
20.02.82: peaked at no.**11**

Blondie's first compilation album was released with two different titles and with two different track listings.

The album was titled *THE BEST OF BLONDIE* in most countries, but was released as *BLONDIE'S HITS* in Germany and the Netherlands.

The North American edition included *One Way Or Another*, which had been released as a single there, while the international edition included the hits *Denis*, *Picture This* and *Union City Blue*, none of which had been issued as a single in North America.

Producer Mike Chapman specially remixed four songs for the compilation: *Heart Of Glass*, *In The Flesh*, *Sunday Girl* and *Rapture*.

THE BEST OF gave Blondie their first no.1 album in Australia and New Zealand, but it wasn't as popular in other countries, charting at no.4 in the UK, no.11 in Zimbabwe, no.30 in the United States and no.34 in Japan. *BLONDIE'S HITS* was a minor no.46 in the Netherlands, but it failed to chart in Germany.

The compilation was accompanied by a video release, which included the following promos:

Call Me/In The Flesh/X Offender/Denis/Detroit 442/(I'm Always Touched By Your) Presence Dear/Picture This/Hanging On The Telephone/Heart Of Glass/Dreaming/ Union City Blue/Atomic/The Tide Is High/Rapture/Sunday Girl

8 ~ THE HUNTER

Orchid Club/Island Of Lost Souls/Dragonfly/For Your Eyes Only/The Beast/War Child/Little Caesar/Danceway/(Can I) Find The Right Words (To Say)/English Boys/The Hunter Gets Captured By The Game

Produced by Mike Chapman.

USA: Chrysalis CHR 1384 (1982).

19.06.82: 58-39-35-**33-33**-70

UK: Chrysalis CDL 1384 (1982).

5.06.82: **9-9**-19-22-40-52-52-68-56-77-77-94

Australia
28.06.82: peaked at no.**15**, charted for 1 weeks

Finland
06.82: **29**

Germany
28.06.82: 53-**49**

Japan
21.06.82: peaked at no.**53**, charted for 6 weeks

Netherlands
12.06.82: 26-**19**-28-45

New Zealand
15.08.82: 29-**27**-42-44

Norway
12.06.82: 34-40-32-32-38-37-24-**19**-26-31-34-34

Sweden
15.06.82: 23-**18** (bi-weekly)

Blondie's sixth studio album was recorded in December 1981 at New York City's The Hit Factory, and was the band's fourth album to be produced by Mike Chapman. As the title *THE HUNTER* suggests, the album loosely focussed on the theme of searching and hunting.

Debbie Harry didn't want to do another Blondie album, and had to be persuaded to do so by Chris Stein; without her, in the eyes of the record company and the band's fans, there was no Blondie.

Debbie and Chris wrote one track on the album, *For Your Eyes Only*, for the 1981 James Bond movie with the same title. However, the film's producers preferred a similarly titled song composed by Bill Conti and Michael Leeson, which Blondie were asked to record. Blondie declined, so the Conti/Leeson song was passed to Sheena Easton, and Blondie recorded their own version of *For Your Eyes Only* for *THE HUNTER*.

THE HUNTER also included a cover of Smokey Robinson's *The Hunter Gets Captured By The Game*, which was originally recorded by The Marvelettes in 1967.

'We identified as both hunter and the hunted,' said Debbie, 'but obviously we were more of the hunted at that point. We were really marked for slaughter and decimated by a bunch of different people right around then, as we had some really bad business problems.'

Two singles were released from the album, *Island Of Lost Souls* and *War Child*, but neither matched the success of the band's previous singles. Similarly, *THE HUNTER* was less well received than previous Blondie albums, and it charted at no.9 in the UK, no.15 in Australia, no.18 in Sweden, no.19 in the Netherlands and Norway, no.27 in New Zealand, no.29 in Finland, no.33 in the United States, no.49 in Germany and no.53 in Japan.

Blondie promoted *THE HUNTER* on their Tracks Across America '82 tour but, like the album, the tour wasn't especially successful and as a result the band's planned autumn tour of Europe was cancelled.

'The record company just didn't market it,' said Debbie, referring to *THE HUNTER*. 'All of our records were different from what they expected. Every time we handed in a record, they'd say, "Uh, we don't hear any singles on this" and hand it back. We handed them *PARALLEL LINES*, which ultimately had six singles worldwide on it, but they handed it back and said they didn't hear any singles on it. *AUTOAMERICAN*, which had *Rapture* and *The Tide Is High* on it was the same way.'

Six months after *THE HUNTER* was released, Blondie split.

'I knew that we were in a different and far less accessible artistic space,' producer Mike Chapman wrote in the liner notes of the 2001 release, 'and that worried me. I could tell things were different now, and I knew that this would be the last Blondie album.'

THE HUNTER was remastered and reissued in 1994, and again in 2001, each time with the same bonus track:

- *War Child (Extended Version)*

THE HUNTER wasn't the last Blondie album, but it was the band's last studio album for 17 years.

the beat!
Trouser Press
JIM MORRISON
Words and photos from a new book
DAVE EDMUNDS
Fifteen years of rock 'n' roll
HAIRCUT 100
The sound of young England
CDC00345
SEPT. 1982 No. 77 $1.50
UK 85p Canada $1.75
BLONDIE
In their own words

9 ~ ROCKBIRD

I Want You/French Kissin' In The USA/Buckle Up/In Love With Love/You Got Me In Trouble/Free To Fall/Rockbird/Secret Life/Beyond The Limit

Produced by Seth Justman.

USA: Geffen Records 9-24123-2 (1986).

11.01.87: 100-100-**97-97**

UK: Chrysalis CCD 1540 (1986).

29.11.86: **31**-32-50-57-63-67-58-60-56-97-95

Australia
16.02.87: peaked at no.**18**, charted for 12 weeks

Sweden
14.01.87: 36-**30**-45 (bi-weekly)

Four years after Blondie split, Debbie Harry released her second solo album, *ROCKBIRD*. An album might have appeared sooner, but Debbie's boyfriend Chris Stein was diagnosed with a serious, life-threatening illness, so she put her career on hold while she was caring for him.

ROCKBIRD was produced by Seth Justman, a member of the J. Geils Band, who also co-wrote three of the album's nine tracks with Debbie. Debbie co-wrote a further three tracks with

Chris Stein, plus one with Nile Rodgers and one with Toni C.. The ninth track, *French Kissin' In The USA* (or simply *French Kissin'*) was composed by Chuck Lorre.

The sleeve design came with the lettering in one of four colours: green, orange, pink or yellow.

Three singles were released from *ROCKBIRD*:

- *French Kissin'*
- *Free To Fall*
- *In Love With Love*

French Kissin' became Debbie's most successful solo single, but *Free To Fall* and *In Love With Love* were only minor hits, and failed to achieve Top 40 status anywhere.

ROCKBIRD achieved no.18 in Australia, no.30 in Sweden and no.31 in the UK, and peaked at a lowly no.97 in the United States.

10 ~ DEF DUMB & BLONDE

I Want That Man/Lovelight/Kiss It Better/Bike Boy/Get Your Way/Maybe For Sure/I'll Never Fall In Love/Calmarie/Sweet And Low/He Is So/Bugeye/Comic Books/Forced To Live/Brite Side/End Of The Run

Bike Boy & Comic Books only featured on the Cassette & CD versions of the album, while *I'll Never Fall In Love & Forced To Live* only featured on the CD version.

Produced by Mike Chapman, except *I Want That Man & Kiss It Better* by Tom Bailey & Eric Thorngren, *Sweet And Low* by Chris Stein, Toni C. & Deborah Harry, and *Brite Side* by Chris Stein & Deborah Harry.

USA: Sire/Red Eye/Reprise Records W2 25938 (1989).

DEF DUMB & BLONDE failed to enter the Top 100 on the Billboard 200 in the United States, however, it did spend eight weeks between positions 101-200, peaking at no.123.

UK: Chrysalis CCD 1650 (1989).

28.10.89: **12**-21-26-29-45-60-67

Australia
4.12.89: peaked at no.**10**, charted for 25 weeks

New Zealand
4.03.90: 47-33-**9**-12-24-22-31-45-45

For her third solo album, *DEF DUMB & BLONDE*, Debbie Harry became Deborah Harry. She co-wrote seven of the 15 tracks on the CD version of the album with Chris Stein, who was solely responsible for composing *Lovelight*.

Deborah co-wrote *Kiss It Better* with Tom Bailey & Alannah Currie, *Calmarie* with Mario Tolédo & Naná Vasconcelos, *Sweet And Low* with Toni C., and *Forced To Live* with Lee Foxx. *I Want That Man* was written by Tom Bailey & Alannah Currie, *I'll Never Fall In Love* was written by Walter Ward & Thomas Bush, and Armand, Miki & Paul Zone composed *Comic Books*.

The album's original title was 'Dream Season', but Deborah changed it to *DEF DUMB & BLONDE* as she felt Dream Season was too similar to Pat Benatar's 1988 album, *WIDE AWAKE IN DREAMLAND*.

Four singles were released from the album:

- *I Want That Man*
- *Brite Side*
- *Sweet And Low*
- *Maybe For Sure*

I Want That Man and *Sweet And Low* both achieved Top 40 status, but *Brite Side* and *Maybe For Sure* were less successful.

DEF DUMB & BLONDE charted at no.9 in New Zealand, no.10 in Australia and no.12 in the UK, but was only a minor hit in the United States, and failed to chart in most countries.

11 ~ THE COMPLETE PICTURE – THE VERY BEST OF DEBORAH HARRY AND BLONDIE

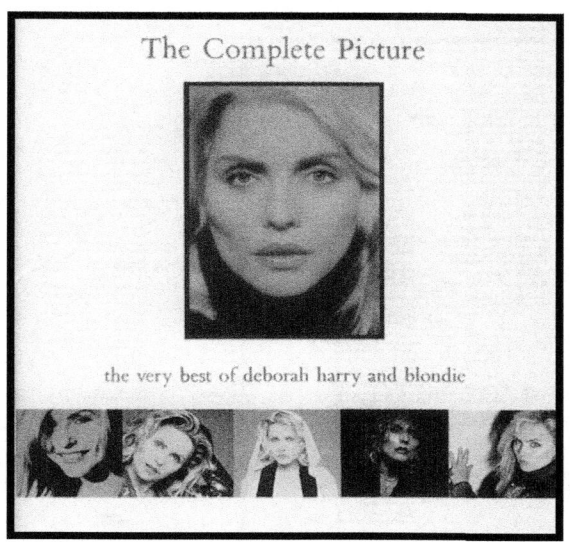

LP1: *Heart Of Glass/I Want That Man/Call Me/Sunday Girl/French Kissin' In The USA/Denis/Rapture/Brite Side/(I'm Always Touched By Your) Presence Dear/Well, Did You Evah!*

LP2: *The Tide Is High/In Love With Love/Hanging On The Telephone/Island Of Lost Souls/Picture This/Dreaming/Sweet And Low/Union City Blue/Atomic/Rip Her To Shreds*

USA: not released.

UK: Chrysalis CHR 1817 (1991).

16.03.91: 5-**3**-**3**-6-10-8-10-15-17-23-27-40-46-50-48-60-59-65-60-61-68-72
29.05.93: 78

Australia
22.04.91: peaked at no.**9**, charted for 19 weeks

Netherlands
30.03.91: 94-64-46-**42**-50-57-85

New Zealand
12.05.91: 19-14-5-3-2-**1**-**1**-2-2-2-3-3-7-7-5-8-12-14-16-23-36-31-39

This compilation, which was released as a double album and a single CD, brought together a selection of 20 hits by both Deborah Harry solo and Blondie.

The Complete Picture

the very best
of deborah harry and blondie

PG

Surprisingly, *THE COMPLETE PICTURE* wasn't released in North America, but it was released in most other regions. The compilation topped the chart in New Zealand for two weeks, and achieved no.3 in the UK, no.9 in Australia and no.42 in the Netherlands.

A similarly titled video compilation was issued at the same time, however, as no promos existed *Rip Her To Shreds* and *Sunday Girl* were omitted. The video compilation included a few hits that were left off the album version, including Deborah's *Backfired* and *Free To Fall*.

The promos featured on video compilation were as follows:

Heart Of Glass/I Want That Man/Denis/Call Me/French Kissin In The USA/Hanging On The Telephone/Sweet And Low/The Tide Is High/In Love With Love/(I'm Always Touched By Your) Presence Dear/Brite Side/Picture This/Rapture/Backfired/Now I Know You Know/Free To Fall/The Hardest Part/Detroit 442/Atomic/Union City Blue/Dreaming/Island Of Lost Souls/Well, Did You Evah!

12 ~ DEBRAVATION

I Can See Clearly/Stability/Strike Me Pink/Rain/Communion/Lip Service/Mood Ring/Keep On Going/Dancing Down The Moon/Standing In My Way/The Fugitive/Dog Star Girl

North America Bonus Tracks: *My Last Date (With You)/Tear Drops*

Chris Stein produced *Stability, Dancing Down The Moon, The Fugitive* & *Dog Star Girl*, Chris Stein & Jon Astley produced *Rain*, Jon Astley produced *Keep On Going*, Anne Dudley produced *Strike Me Pink* & *Mood Ring*, Arthur Baker produced *I Can See Clearly*, Guy Pratt produced *Communion*, Toni C. produced *Lip Service*, John Williams produced *Standing In My Way*, Andy Paley & R.E.M produced *My Last Date (With You)*, and Andy Paley produced *Tear Drops*.

USA: Sire/Reprise Records 0 45303-2 (1993).

DEBRAVATION wasn't a hit in the United States.

UK: Chrysalis CDCHR 6033 (1993).

31.07.93: **24**-55

Deborah co-wrote eight of the twelve tracks that featured on her fourth solo album, *DEBRAVATION*, the exceptions being *I Can See Clearly*, *Rain*, *Keep On Going* and *Dog Star Girl*.

The North American edition of the album included two bonus tracks, one of which ~ *My Last Date (With You)* ~ was co-produced by R.E.M, who also played instrumental backing on the recording.

Two singles were lifted from the album, *I Can See Clearly* and *Strike Me Pink*. The former achieved Top 40 status in the UK, but the latter was only a minor hit ~ not helped by the controversial music video, which was banned in many countries due to its disturbing content: as Deborah sits watching, a glass tank fills with water, drowning the man inside the tank.

Like *I Can See Clearly*, the only country where *DEBRAVATION* entered the Top 40 was the UK, where it made its debut at no.24 but slipped out of the chart after just two weeks.

Deborah's fifth and most recent solo album, *NECESSARY EVIL*, was released in September 2007. It was a minor no.86 hit in the UK, but failed to chart anywhere else.

13 ~ BEAUTIFUL – THE REMIX ALBUM

USA: *Heart Of Glass (Richie Jones Club Mix)/Dreaming (The Sub-Urban Dream Mix)/ One Way Or Another (Damien's Supermarket Mix)/Atomic (Diddy's 12" Mix)/Rapture (K-Klassic Mix)/The Tide Is High (Sand Dollar Mix)/Heart Of Glass (MK 12" Mix)/Call Me (E-Smoove's Beat Vocal Mix)/Dreaming (Utah Saints Mix)/Atomic (Armand's Short Circuit Mix)/Fade Away And Radiate (108 BPM Mix)*

UK: *Union City Blue (Diddy's Power And Passion Mix)/Dreaming (Utah Saints Mix)/ Rapture (K-Klassic Radio Mix)/Heart Of Glass (Diddy's Adorable Illusion Mix)/Sunday Girl (Hardly Handbag Mix)/Call Me (Debbie Does Dallas)/Atomic (Diddy's 12" Mix)/The Tide Is High (Sand Dollar Mix)/Hanging On The Telephone (Nose Bleed Handbag Mix)/ Fade Away And Radiate (108 BPM Mix)/Dreaming (The Sub-Urban Dream Mix)/Atomic (Armand's Short Circuit Mix)*

USA: Chrysalis F2-32748 (1995).

THE REMIX PROJECT – REMIXED REMADE REMODELED didn't chart in the United States.

UK: Chrysalis CDCHR 6105 (1995).

29.07.95: **25**-47-81

BEAUTIFUL – THE REMIX ALBUM was titled *THE REMIX PROJECT – REMIXED REMADE REMODELED* in North America, where the album was released with a completely different track listing.

The album made its chart debut at no.25 in the UK, but climbed no higher, and only charted for three weeks. The album failed to chart at all anywhere else.

Three singles were issued from *BEAUTIFUL – THE REMIX ALBUM*:

- *Atomic '94*
- *Heart Of Glass '95*
- *Union City Blue '95*

Atomic '94 and *Heart Of Glass '95* both entered the Top 20 in the UK, where *Union City Blue '95* also achieved Top 40 status ~ but, like the album, the singles didn't do anything in other countries.

In 2002, *BEAUTIFUL – THE REMIX ALBUM* was reissued by the budget label Disky in the Netherlands.

14 ~ ATOMIC – THE VERY BEST OF

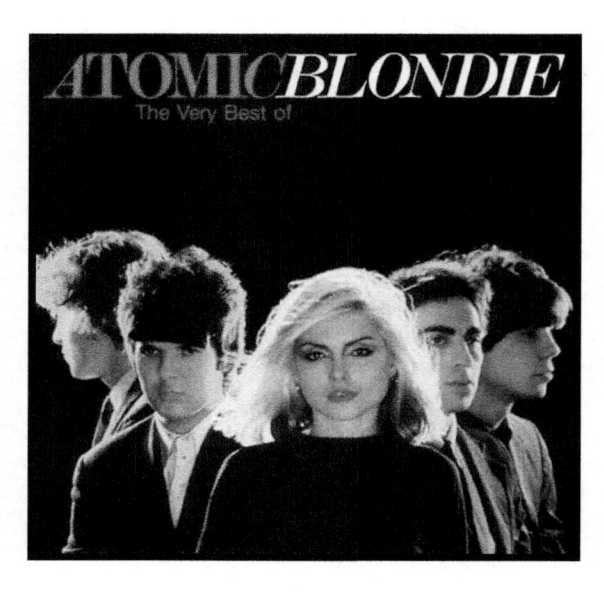

Atomic/Heart Of Glass/Sunday Girl/Call Me/The Tide Is High/Denis/Dreaming/Rapture/ Hanging On The Telephone/(I'm Always Touched By Your) Presence Dear/Island Of Lost Souls/Picture This/Union City Blue/War Child/Rip Her To Shreds/One Way Or Another/ X Offender/I'm Gonna Love You Too/Fade Away And Radiate

Bonus Tracks: *Atomic '98 (Xenomania Mix)/(Tall Paul Remix)*

USA: not released.

UK: Chrysalis 7243 4 94996 2 1 (1998).

25.07.98: **12**-15-14-20-24-31-39-47-54-64-74-63-65-86
20.02.99: 14-12-13-18-23-32-40-51-55-57-60-69-55-46-52-60-63-86-67-76-x-89-89
16.10.99: 79-91
15.09.01: 94-86-93-x-42-48-69-83
12.01.02: 76-86-82-82-88-99-x-x-x-x-x-x-x-100
28.09.02: 79

Netherlands
4.09.99: 59-**48**-57-78

New Zealand
9.09.01: 22-**18**-23-42-48

The release of *ATOMIC – THE VERY BEST OF* coincided with the members of Blondie getting back together, and the start of what proved to be a very successful comeback tour.

The compilation, which was passed over for release in North America, charted at no.12 in the UK, no.18 in New Zealand and no.48 in the Netherlands, but missed the chart in most countries.

Twelve months after the compilation's original release, it was reissued as a 2CD set, with a bonus CD, and titled *ATOMIC/ATOMIX – THE VERY BEST OF*. The tracks on the second CD were as follows:

Atomic (Diddy's 12" Mix)/Dreaming (Utah Saints Mix)/Denis (Danny D. Remix)/ Call Me (Original 12" Version)/Heart Of Glass (Original 12" Instrumental)/Rapture (US Disco Version)/War Child (12" Version)/Atomic '98 (Dana Intellectual Mix)/ Sunday Girl (French Version).

The mixes of *Call Me*, *Heart Of Glass* and *Rapture*, plus *Atomic '98*, hadn't previously been released on CD.

ATOMIC – THE VERY BEST OF was reissued in 2011, with the compilation's original track listing, but re-packaged and re-titled, *ESSENTIAL*.

MOJO

The Music Magazine

FEBRUARY 1999 · £3.10

Nick Drake — Inside the mind of a boy genius

Hail Elvis — King of rock? Sultan of *soul*!

The Beatles — That rooftop 'audition' relived

B*ll*cks! — At last, the punk box set

NEW YORK NAKED CITY SPECIAL

THEY'RE BACK!
BLONDIE
The pop-art project that ate the world... *twice*

THE VELVET UNDERGROUND
Sex, drugs and paranoia: John Cale confesses all

15 ~ NO EXIT

Produced by Craig Leon.

Screaming Skin/Forgive And Forget (Pull Down The Night)/Maria/No Exit/Double Take/ Nothing Is Real But The Girl/Boom Boom In The Zoom Zoom Room/Night Wind Sent/ Under The Gun (For Jeffrey Lee Pierce)/Out In The Streets/Happy Dog (For Caggy)/The Dream's Lost On Me/Diving/Dig Up The Conjo

North America Bonus Tracks: *Dreaming (Live)/Call Me (Live)/Rapture (Live)*

UK/Europe Bonus Tracks: *Rapture (Live)/Heart Of Glass (Live)*

Australia Bonus Tracks: *Call Me (Live)/Rapture (Live)/Heart Of Glass (Live)*

Japan Bonus Track: *Hot Shot*

Limited Edition Bonus EP: *Call Me (Live)/Rapture (Live)/Dreaming (Live)/Heart Of Glass (Live)*

USA: Beyond 63985-78003-2 (1999).

13.03.99: **18**-28-41-58-75-80-86-87-92

UK: Beyond/Epic 5014082 (1999).

27.02.99: **3**-8-13-21-25-34-38-47-60-72-81-98-80-89-75-68-64-53-69

BLONDIE
NO EXIT
INCLUYE EL SUPERHIT
MARIA
BLONDIE
NO EXIT
BMG

Australia
?.99: peaked at no.**72**

Austria
28.02.99: 41-x-32-25-23-24-24-21-**20**-21-29-29-24-**20**-38-42

Belgium
10.04.99: 48-**45**

France
7.02.99: 56-**25**-28-32-36-53-70-66

Germany
22.02.99: 26-22-26-31-23-23-**18**-**18**-20-**18**-26-24-30-32-45-53-54-70-71-71-83-89-92

Netherlands
17.04.99: 100-91-82-**80**-90-94-90

Sweden
4.03.99: 56-54-45-48-x-54-**36**-39-42-55-57

Switzerland
21.02.99: 27-24-22-**21**-24-**21**-24-22-25-22-33-34-36-33-38-39-46

NO EXIT was Blondie's seventh studio album, and the band's first since *THE HUNTER* was released in 1982.

The album was released in several different formats, with different bonus tracks featuring on editions issued in different regions. The album was also released with a second, limited edition CD. The live bonus tracks featured on the various releases were all recorded at London's Lyceum Ballroom on 22nd November 1998.

Blondie worked with Mike Chapman, who had produced the band's most recent studio albums, on the early demos for the album that became *NO EXIT*, but the album was produced by Craig Leon.

'The title,' said Chris Stein, 'was taken from a Sartre play, which says there's no madness in individuals, it's all in groups.'

Deborah Harry described *No Exit* as 'a real combo effort – it was Jimmy (Destri) and Chris and Romy (Ashby) and me. Jimmy wrote a couple of verses of a gangsta rap and I said, Jimmy, I can't be a gansta rapper! That would really be tasteless and unethical. So he says, okay, let's make it a Gothic rap about a vampire on the scene. That worked a lot better.'

NO EXIT, for the most part, was written by members of the band, but it did include one cover version, *Out In The Streets*, which was composed by Jeff Barry and Ellie Greenwich, and originally recorded by The Shangri-Las for their 1965 album, *65!*.

Blondie recorded a demo of *Out In The Streets* in 1975, before the band secured a recording contract ~ the demo was released in 1994, on the 2CD compilation, *THE PLATINUM COLLECTION*.

NO EXIT charted at no.3 in the UK, no.10 in Ireland, no.18 in Germany and the UK, no.20 in Austria, no.21 in Switzerland, no.25 in France and no.36 in Sweden, but was only a minor hit in Australia, Belgium and the Netherlands.

Three singles were lifted from the album:

- *Maria*
- *Nothing Is Real But The Girl*
- *No Exit*

Maria gave Blondie their sixth no.1 single in the UK, and came exactly 20 years after their first chart topper, *Heart Of Glass*. *No Exit* was only released as a limited edition single in Europe, but it wasn't a hit anywhere.

NO EXIT was reissued in 2001 with three bonus tracks:

- *Hot Shot*
- *Rapture (Live)*
- *Heart Of Glass (Live)*

16 ~ GREATEST HITS

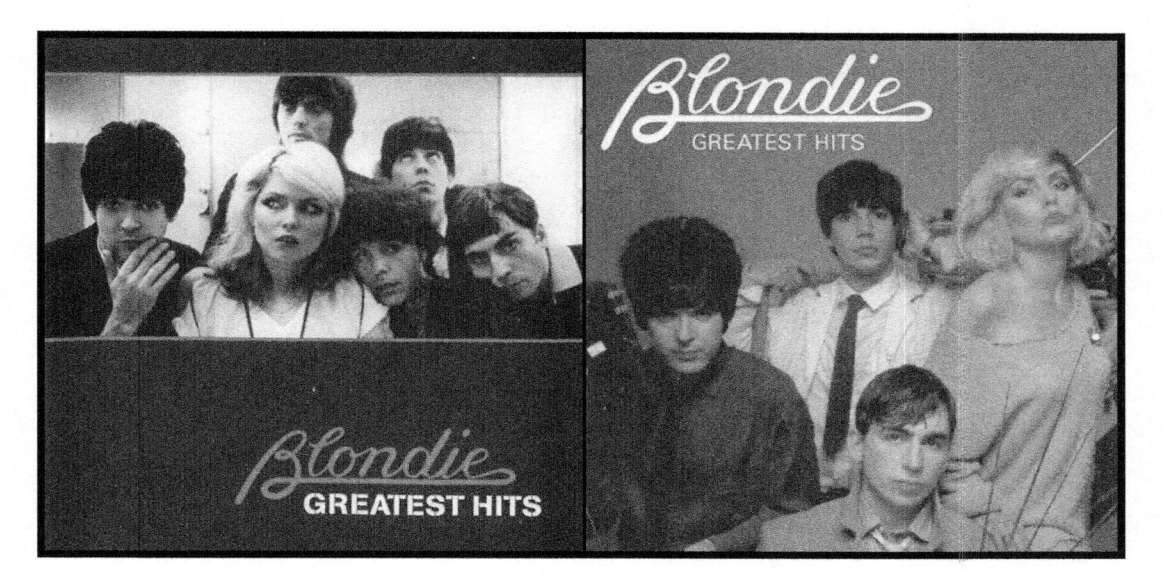

Dreaming/Call Me/One Way Or Another/Heart Of Glass (Special Mix)/The Tide Is High/ X Offender/Hanging On The Telephone/Rip Her To Shreds/Rapture (Special Mix)/Atomic/ Picture This/In The Flesh (Special Mix)/Denis/(I'm Always Touched By Your) Presence Dear/ Union City Blue/The Hardest Part/Island Of Lost Souls/Sunday Girl (Special Mix)/Maria

USA: Capitol Records/Chrysalis 72435-42068-2-5 (2002).

GREATEST HITS wasn't a hit in the United States.

UK: Capitol Records/Chrysalis 72435-42068-2-5 (2002).

2.11.02: **38**-40-52-60-86-x-x-97
27.03.04: 95-82
25.06.05: 77-97
27.10.06: 97-x-100
2.03.13: 99-91-81-71

Australia
10.08.03: **73**

New Zealand
17.08.03: 37-20-**15**-19-19-17-33-39

Sweden
30.01.03: 50-45-**30**-59

GREATEST HITS was the first Blondie compilation to be digitally remastered, the first to be officially approved by the band since 1981's *THE BEST OF BLONDIE*, and the first to feature the band's comeback single, *Maria*.

Maria apart, the tracks featured on *GREATEST HITS* mirrored those on *THE BEST OF BLONDIE*, including producer Mike Chapman's 'special' mixes of *Heart Of Glass*, *Rapture*, *In The Flesh* and *Sunday Girl*.

The album charted at no.15 in New Zealand, no.30 in Sweden and no.38 in the UK, was a minor hit in Australia, but failed to chart in many countries.

GREATEST HITS, like *THE BEST OF BLONDIE* before it, was accompanied by a video album, released on DVD as *Greatest Video Hits*. The DVD featured the same promos as the 1981 release, with three music videos added:

- *The Hardest Part*
- *Island Of Lost Souls*
- *Maria*

The DVD featured the original, uncensored version of *Maria*.

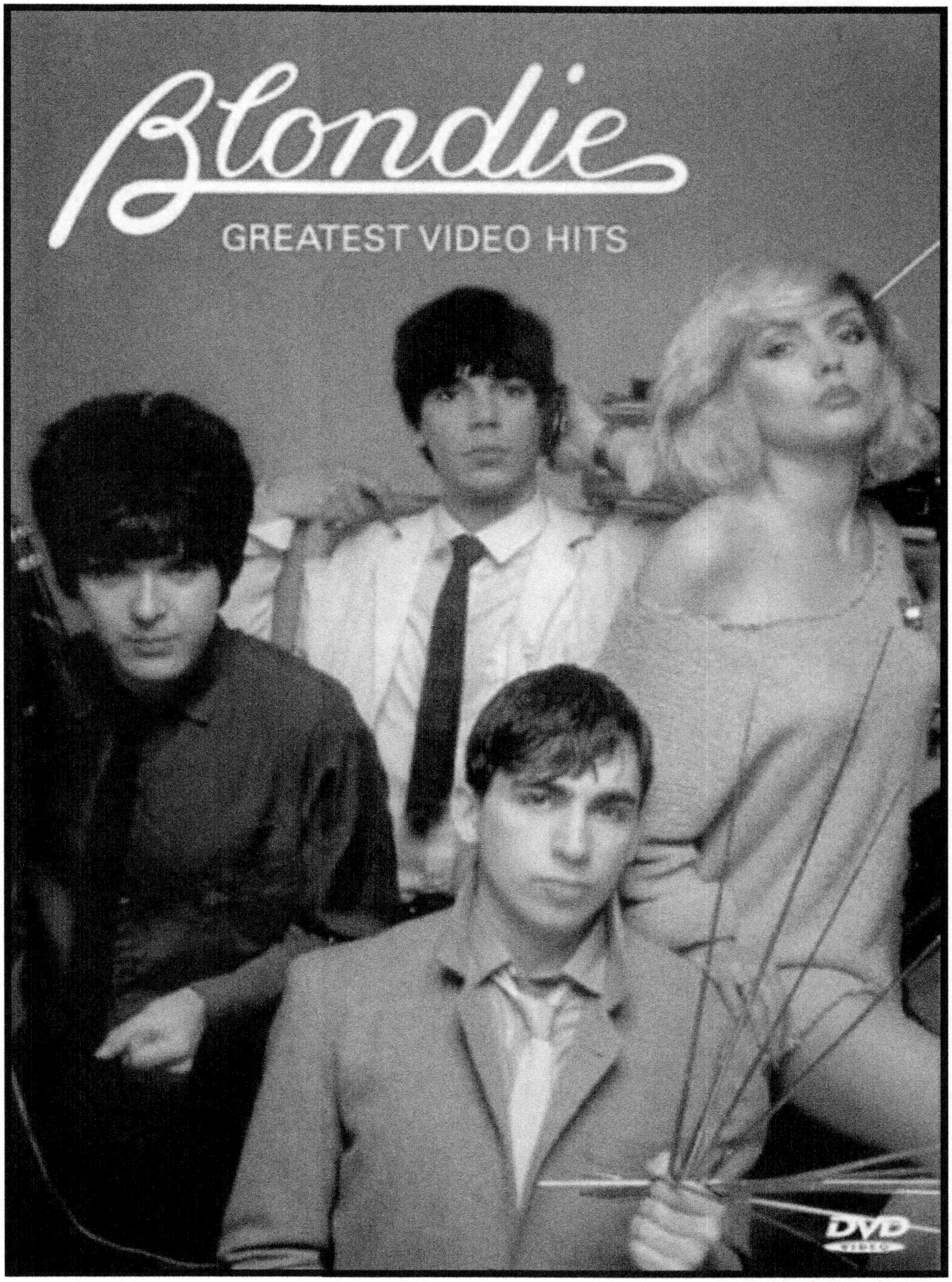
Blondie
GREATEST VIDEO HITS
DVD

17 ~ THE CURSE OF BLONDIE

Produced by Steve Thompson & Jeff Bova.

Shakedown/Good Boys/Undone/Golden Rod/Rules For Living/Background Melody (The Only One)/Magic (Asadoya Yunta)/End To End/Hello Joe/The Tingler/Last One In The World/Diamond Bridge/Desire Brings Me Back/Song For Love (For Richard)

USA Bonus Track: *Good Boys (Video)*.

UK/Europe Bonus Track: *Good Boys (Giorgio Moroder Single Mix)*.

Japan Bonus Tracks: *The Tide Is High (Live)/Rapture (Live)*.

USA: Sanctuary Records 06076-84666-2 (2003).

THE CURSE OF BLONDIE failed to enter the Top 100 of the Billboard 200 in the United States, but it did spend a solitary week at no.160.

UK: Epic 511921 9 (2003).

25.10.03: **36**-78

Australia
5.10.03: **83**

Germany
20.10.03: **84**

THE CURSE OF BLONDIE was the band's eighth studio album, and was four years in the making. Early demos, recorded with producer Craig Leon, went missing from the band's luggage at a UK airport. The tracks had to be re-recorded, this time with producer Steve Thompson, with the exception of *Good Boys*, which Jeff Bova produced.

The album was issued with different bonus tracks in different territories. The live versions of *The Tide Is High* and *Rapture* included on Japanese pressings were official bootlegs recorded during Blondie's appearance at Summer Sonic 03, a rock festival simultaneously staged at Chiba and Osaka, Japan.

THE CURSE OF BLONDIE charted at no.36 in the UK, but failed to achieve Top 40 status anywhere else ~ it was a minor hit in Australia, Germany and the United States, but didn't chart in most countries.

Good Boys, the track produced by Jeff Bova, was the only single lifted from the album. It sold well enough to achieve Top 40 status, but it wasn't a major hit.

Blondie fans had to wait another eight years for a new studio album, *PANIC OF GIRLS*, which was a minor hit in the Netherlands and the UK, but became the band's first album to fail to achieve Top 40 status anywhere.

LIMITED EDITION COLLECTOR'S PACK
BLONDIE
free BLONDIE photo supplement by Chris Stein exclusive to hmv
DELUXE EDITION
11 BRAND NEW SONGS
+2 BONUS TRACKS
panic of girls / blondie
PACK INCLUDES
100% official 132-page magazine!
"Call Me"
6 pin badges!
Giant double -sided poster!
4 postcards shot by Chris Stein!
ALL-NEW INTERVIEWS! CLASSIC PICS! TRACK BY TRACK!
Future
ISBN 1-858703-88-

18 ~ GREATEST HITS: SOUND + VISION

CD: *Heart Of Glass/Sunday Girl/Atomic/Call Me/The Tide Is High/Rapture/Maria/In The Flesh (Remix)/X Offender/Rip Her To Shreds/Denis/(I'm Always Touched By Your) Presence Dear/Picture This/Fade Away And Radiate/Hanging On The Telephone/One Way Or another/Dreaming/Union City Blue/Island Of Lost Souls/Good Boys (Blow-Up Mix)/ End To End/Rapture Riders*

X Offender and *(I'm Always Touched By Your) Presence Dear* were omitted from the international edition.

DVD: *In The Flesh/X Offender/Denis/Detroit 442/(I'm Always Touched By Your) Presence Dear/Picture This/Hanging On The Telephone/Heart Of Glass/Dreaming/The Hardest Part/Union City Blue/Atomic/The Tide Is High/Rapture/Island Of Lost Souls/Maria/Good Boys/Rapture Riders (UK Version)*

X Offender and *(I'm Always Touched By Your) Presence Dear* were omitted from the international edition, and *Rapture Riders (UK Version)* was omitted from the UK edition.

USA: Capitol Records/EMI 09463-45863-20 (2006).

GREATEST HITS: SOUND & VISION wasn't a hit in the United States.

UK: EMI/Chrysalis/Capitol Records 0946 345054 2 0 (2005).

19.11.05: **48**-62-65-65-66-62-67
11.08.07: 97-86-92-x-x-x-78-79-94-97-99

Norway
6.09.08: **23**-23-32-35

Spain
1.10.06: **81**-94
25.01.09: 85

This compilation, Blondie's first to be released as a CD/DVD package, was first issued in the UK in November 2005 titled *GREATEST HITS*, but with a 'Sight + Sound' sticker on the cover. The package wasn't released internationally until the following March, when it was re-titled *GREATEST HITS: SIGHT + SOUND*.
    As well as the usual hits, the compilation was notable for the inclusion of *Rapture Raiders*, a mash-up of Blondie's *Rapture* and *Riders On The Storm* by The Doors.
    GREATEST HITS: SIGHT + SOUND charted at no.23 in Norway and no.48 in the UK, and was a minor hit in Spain, but it failed to chart in most countries.

19 ~ BLONDIE 4(0) EVER

GREATEST HITS: DELUXE REDUX

Heart Of Glass/Dreaming/The Tide Is High/Maria/Sunday Girl/Hanging On The Telephone/Rapture/One Way Or Another/Call Me/Atomic/Rip Her To Shreds

GHOSTS OF DOWNLOAD

Sugar On The Side/Rave/A Rose By Any Name/Winter/I Want To Drag You Around/I Screwed Up/Relax/Take Me In The Night/Make A Way/Mile High/Euphoria/Take It Back/ Backroom

Digital Bonus Tracks: *Put Some Color On You/Can't Stop Wanting/Prism*

Bonus DVD: Live At CBGB 1977 (Deluxe Edition): *Kung Fu Girls/In The Sun/Little Girl Lies/Look Good In Blue/Man Overboard/A Shark In Jets Clothing/Rifle Range/In The Flesh/X Offender/Youth Nabbed As A Sniper/Rip Her To Shreds/Heart Full Of Soul/I Love Playing With Fire/Palisades Park/Denis (Rehearsal)*

Produced by Jeff Saltzman.

USA: Five Seven Music NBL 500-2 (2014).

BLONDIE 4(0) EVER failed to enter the Top 100 in the United States, but it did spend one week at no.109, before falling off the Billboard 200 the following week.

UK: Noble ID 500-2 (2014).

24.05.14: **16**-67

Australia
8.06.14: **72**

Germany
30.05.14: **44**

Blondie started work on their tenth studio album soon after their ninth, *PANIC OF GIRLS*, was released.

'It's been like two years that I have been working on this,' said Chris Stein. 'This one is more computer-based than the last record, which was more band-based. A lot of the programmed parts remained on the record, more so than the previous records.'

The new songs were recorded at New York City's Mercy Sound Recording Studios and Skyline Studios in Oakland, California.

'It's always the music,' said Deborah Harry, 'the music is the inspiration. Every piece has its own mood, its own arc, and a lot of times the lyrics sort of suggest themselves.'

The new album was titled *GHOSTS OF DOWNLOAD*, which Chris Stein explained referred to 'all spirits in the background of electricity and data'.

To celebrate the band's 40th anniversary, Blondie decided to re-record some of their hits, and release the new album as a double album, titled *BLONDIE 4(0) EVER*. As well as *GHOSTS OF DOWNLOAD*, the package included a greatest hits CD titled *GREATEST HITS: DELUXE REDUX*, with 10 of the 11 featured hits newly recorded, the one exception being the band's most recent hit, *Maria*.

The Deluxe Edition of *BLONDIE 4(0) EVER* came with a bonus DVD, which showcased the band live at New York City's CBGB music club in 1977, plus a 1979 concert poster and five postcards featuring photographs by Chris Stein.

BLONDIE 4(0) EVER achieved no.16 in the UK and no.44 in Germany, but it was only a minor hit in Australia and the United States, and failed to chart in most countries.

Three singles, which all failed to chart anywhere, were released from *GHOSTS OF DOWNLOAD*:

- *A Rose By Any Name*
- *Sugar On The Side*
- *I Want To Drag You Around*

The distinctive artwork for *A Rose By Any Name* and *Sugar On The Side* was the work of the former DC Comics artist, J.H. Williams III, who was also responsible for the *GHOSTS OF DOWNLOAD* sleeve design.

THE SUNDAY TIMES *magazine*

"Would I be naked on stage now? Probably"

Blondie's Debbie Harry on exhibitionism, sex in her seventies and the search for her real mother

20 ~ POLLINATOR

Doom Or Destiny/Long Time/Already Naked/Fun/My Monster/Best Day Ever/Gravity/When I Gave Up On You/Love Level/Too Much/Fragments/(Silence)

CD Bonus Track: *Tonight*

Japan Bonus Tracks: *The Breaks/Fun (Greg Cohen Spirit Of 79 Remix)/(Eric Kupper Disco Remix)/(Drew G Remix)*

Produced by John Congleton.

USA: BMG 538263540 (2017).

27.05.17: **63**

UK: BMG 538263540 (2017).

18.05.17: **4**-19-44-66-x-98

Australia
21.05.17: **29**

Austria
19.05.17: **27**-73

Belgium
13.05.17: **55**

France
13.05.17: **69**

Germany
1.05.17: **21**-69

Netherlands
13.05.17: **78**

Spain
14.05.17: **86**

Switzerland
14.05.17: **22**-86-96

Blondie's eleventh and most recent studio, *POLLINATOR*, was released in May 2017, and saw a return to a more band-oriented sound, compared with *GHOSTS OF DOWNLOAD*.

The album was recorded between 2015-17, and was recorded at New York City's The Magic Shop. The album featured a number of collaborations with outside artists, including Johnny Marr, Nick Valensi from The Strokes and Sia.

'We thought to ask people because there's so much good music swirling around,' said Chris Stein. 'We sorted the contributors ourselves, or someone would send us a bunch of songs, and we'd pick one.'

The album also featured backing vocals by Joan Jett on *Doom And Destiny*, by Gregory Roberts on *When I Gave Up On You* and by John Roberts on *Love Level*. *Tonight*, a bonus track on the CD version of the album, featured Laurie Anderson.

In the Summer of 2017, Blondie promoted *POLLINATOR* by co-headlining a tour of the United States with the band Garbage. A beekeeper herself, Deborah Harry chose to highlight the world's declining bee population and environmental concerns by appearing on stage wearing a Honey Bee costume, with a full-length cape that stated: 'STOP F**KING THE PLANET'.

POLLINATOR was generally well received, and sold better than Blondie's most recent albums. The album made its debut at no.4 in the UK, and charted at no.21 in Germany, no.22 in Switzerland, no.27 in Austria and no.29 in Australia. The album was also a minor hit in Belgium, France, the Netherlands, Spain and the United States.

Four singles were released from *POLLINATOR*:

- *Fun*
- *Long Time*
- *Too Much*
- *Doom Or Destiny*

Fun was issued as a limited edition 7" and 12" single in the UK, where it charted at no.2 on the Vinyl Singles chart and no.3 on the Physical Singles chart. *Fun* also went to no.1 on Billboard's Dance Club Songs chart in the United States, however, poor streaming 'sales' meant *Fun* failed to enter any mainstream charts anywhere.

Long Time topped the Vinyl Singles and Physical Singles charts in the UK, and rose to no.5 on Billboard's Dance Club Songs chart in the United States, but like *Fun* a relative lack of streaming 'sales' meant it wasn't a hit on any mainstream charts.

21 ~ AGAINST THE ODDS 1974-1982

Box-set comprising either:

- 3 x CD
- 4 x LP
- 8 x CD (Deluxe Edition)
- 10 x LP, 1 x 10" LP & 7" Single (Super Deluxe Edition)

CD1: *Out In The Streets (1974)/The Disco Song/Sexy Ida/Platinum Blonde/The Thin Line/Puerto Rico/Once I Had A Love (1975)/Out In The Streets/X Offender (Intro)/X Offender (Private Stock Single)/In The Sun (Private Stock Single)/Little Girl Lies (Private Stock Single)/In The Flesh (Extended Intro)/A Shark In Jets Clothing (Take 2)/Kung Fu Girls (Take 8)/Scenery*

CD2: *Denis (Terry Ellis Mix)/Moonlight Drive/Bermuda Triangle Blues – Flight 45 (Take 1)/I Didn't Have The Nerve To Say No (Take 1)/I'm On E (Take 2)/Kidnapper (Take 2)/Detroit 442 (Take 2)/Poets Problem/Once I Had A Love (Mike Chapman Demo)/Sunday Girl (French Version)/I'll Never Break Away From This Heart Of Mine (Pretty Baby)/Hanging On The Telephone (Mike Chapman Demo)/Will Anything Happen (Instrumental)/Call Me/Spaghetti Song (Atomic Part 2)/Die Young Stay Pretty (Take 1)/Underground Girl/Union City Blue (Instrumental)/Llámame*

CD3: *I Love You Honey, Give Me A Beer (Go Through It)/Live It Up (Giorgio Moroder Demo)/Angels On The Balcony (Giorgio Moroder Demo)/The Tide Is High (Demo)/Susie And Jeffrey/Rapture (Disco Version)/Autoamerican Ad/Yuletide Throwdown/War Child (Chris Stein Mix)/Call Me (Chris Stein Mix)/Heart Of Glass (Chris Stein Mix)/Nameless (Home Tape)/Mr*

Sightseer/Sunday Girl (Home Tape)/Theme From Topkapi (Home Tape)/The Hardest Part (Home Tape)/Ring Of Fire (Home Tape)

LP1 ~ Out In The Streets (Out-Takes & Rarities): *Out In The Streets (1974 Session)/The Disco Song (1974 Session)/Sexy Ida (1974 Session)/Platinum Blonde (Betrock Demo)/The Thin Line (Betrock Demo)/Puerto Rico (Betrock Demo)/Out In The Streets (Betrock Demo)/Nameless (Home Tape)/Mr Sightseer/Sunday Girl (Home Tape)/Theme From Topkapi (Home Tape)/The Hardest Part (Home Tape)/Ring Of Fire (Home Tape)*

LP2 ~ Plaza Sound (Out-Takes & Rarities): *X Offender (Intro)/X Offender (Private Stock Single Version)/In The Sun (Private Stock Single Version)/Little Girl Lies (Private Stock Mix)/In The Flesh (Extended Intro)/A Shark In Jets Clothing (Take 2)/Kung Fu Girls (Take 8)/Scenery (Plaza Sound Outtake)/Denis (Terry Ellis Mix)/Bermuda Triangle Blues – Flight 45 ((Take 1)/I Didn't Have The Nerve To Say No (Take 1)/I'm On E (Take 2)/Kidnapper (Take 2)/Detroit 442 (Take 2)/Poet's Problem*

LP3 ~ Parallel Beats (Out-Takes & Rarities): *Once I Had A Love (Mike Chapman Demo)/ Sunday Girl (French Version)/I'll Never Break Away From This Heart Of Mine (Pretty Baby) (Take 1)/Hanging On The Telephone (Mike Chapman Demo)/Will Anything Happen (Instrumental)/Underground Girl/Call Me/Spaghetti Song (Atomic Part 2)/Die Young Stay Pretty (Take 1)/Union City Blue (Instrumental)/Llámame*

LP4 ~ Blondie (Out-Takes & Rarities): *I Love You Honey, Give Me A Beer (Go Through It)/Live It Up (Giorgio Moroder Demo)/Angels On The Balcony (Giorgio Moroder Demo)/The Tide Is High (Demo)/Suzy & Jeffrey/Rapture (Disco Version)/Autoamerican Ad/Yuletide Throwdown*

Deluxe Edition

6 x Blondie albums with bonus tracks, plus 2 x bonus CDs.

BLONDIE
Bonus tracks: *X Offender (Intro)/X Offender (Private Stock Single)/In The Sun (Private Stock Single)/Little Girl Lies ((Private Stock Mix)/In The Flesh (Extended Intro)/A Shark In Jets Clothing (Take 2)/Kung Fu Girls (Take 8)/Scenery*

PLASTIC LETTERS
Bonus tracks: *Denis (Terry Ellis Mix)/Moonlight Drive/Bermuda Triangle Blues – Flight 45 (Take 1)/I Didn't Have The Nerve To Say No (Take 1)/I'm On E (Take 2)/Kidnapper (Take 2)/Detroit 442 (Take 2)/Poets Problem*

PARALLEL LINES
Bonus tracks: *Once I Had A Love (Mike Chapman Demo)/Sunday Girl (French Version)/I'll Never Break Away From This Heart Of Mine (Pretty Baby)/Hanging On The Telephone (Mike Chapman Demo)/Will Anything Happen (Instrumental)*

EAT TO THE BEAT
Bonus tracks: *Call Me/Spaghetti Song/Die Young Stay Pretty (Take 1)/Underground Girl/Union City Blue (Instrumental)/Llámame*

AUTOAMERICAN
Bonus tracks: *Autoamerican Ad/I Love You Honey, Give Me A Beer (Go Through It)/Live It Up (Giorgio Moroder Demo)/Angels On The Balcony (Giorgio Moroder Demo)/The Tide Is High (Demo)/Susie & Jeffrey/Rapture (Disco Version)*

THE HUNTER
Bonus track: *Yuletide Throwdown*

Bonus CD: Out In The Streets (Out-Takes & Rarities)
Out In The Streets (1974 Session)/The Disco Song (1974 Session)/Sexy Ida (1974 Session)/Platinum Blonde (Betrock Demo)/The Thin Line (Betrock Demo)/Puerto Rico (Betrock Demo)/Once I Had A Love (Betrock Demo)/Out In The Streets (Betrock Demo)

Bonus CD: Home Tapes (Out-Takes & Rarities)
Nameless (Home Tape)/Mr Sightseer/Sunday Girl (Home Tape)/Theme From Topkapi (Home Tape)/The Hardest Part (Home Tape)/Ring Of Fire (Home Tape)/Heart Of Glass (Chris Stein Mix)/Call Me (Chris Stein Mix)/War Child (Chris Stein Mix)

Super Deluxe Edition

LP1: *BLONDIE*
LP2: *PLASTIC LETTERS*
LP3: *PARALLEL LINES*
LP4: *EAT TO THE BEAT*

LP5: *AUTOAMERICAN*
LP6: *THE HUNTER*
LP7: Plaza Sound (Out-Takes & Rarities) ~ as above
LP8: Parallel Beats (Out-Takes & Rarities) ~ as above
LP9: Coca Cola (Out-Takes & Rarities) ~ as Blondie (Out-Takes & Rarities) above
LP10: Home Tapes (Out-Takes & Rarities) ~ as Bonus CD above
10" LP: Out In The Streets (Out-Takes & Rarities) ~ as above
7" Single: *Moonlight Drive/Mr Sightseer*

USA & UK: UMC/Chrysalis 00602508761010 (3CD), 00602508760747 (4LP), 00602508760969 (Deluxe Edition), 00602508760693 (Super Deluxe Edition) (2022).

UK
8.09.22: **25**

Belgium
3.09.22: **40**

Germany
8.09.22: **16**

Switzerland
4.09.22: **60**

AGAINST THE ODDS 1974-1982 was a comprehensive box-set that focussed on Blondie's first six studio albums, and was issued in a number of different formats, on both vinyl and CD. The release featured numerous rarities, including demos and outtakes.

'It really is a treat to see how far we have come when I listen to these early attempts to capture our ideas on relatively primitive equipment,' said Deborah Harry. 'Fortunately the essence of being a band in the early seventies held some of the anti-social, counter culture energies of the groups that were the influencers of the sixties. I am excited about this special collection. When I listen to these old tracks, it puts me there like I am a time traveller. As bad as it was sometimes, it was also equally good. No regrets. More music.'

The standard edition was released on three CDs or four vinyl albums, and featured the rarities, but not the six studio albums themselves. The deluxe edition issued on CD, as well as the rarities, featured Blondie's first six studio albums, and came with a 128 page hardback book.

The super deluxe edition, released on vinyl, featured Blondie's first six studio albums, plus five albums ~ one of them 10" ~ of rarities and a bonus 7" single. This edition came with a 144 page hardback book, plus a 120 page photographic discography book. As well as standard black vinyl, the super deluxe edition was pressed on platinum blonde vinyl and on red vinyl, in limited numbers.

Despite the high price, the box-set charted in several countries, and achieved no.16 in Germany, no.25 in the UK, no.40 in Belgium and no.60 in Switzerland.

ONCE MORE INTO THE BLEACH

Debbie Harry
Blondie

Available on Double L.P, Double Cassette & Single C.D.

OUR PRICE music
Mad About Music
SEE A SPECIALIST

THE ALMOST TOP 40 ALBUMS

Only one album, credited to Debbie Harry and Blondie, has made the Top 50 in one or more countries, but failed to enter the Top 40 in any.

ONCE MORE INTO THE BLEACH

This 1988 compilation included remixes of hits by Debbie solo and with Blondie, with the North American, European and UK editions all featuring different track listings. The album charted at no.46 in Australia and no.50 in the UK, but it failed to chart in most countries, and didn't achieve Top 40 status anywhere,

BLONDIE'S TOP 15 ALBUMS

This Top 15 Albums listing has been compiled using the same points system as for Blondie & Deborah Harry's Top 20 Singles listing.

Rank/Album/Points

1 *PARALLEL LINES* ~ 1454 points

2 *EAT TO THE BEAT* ~ 1088 points

3 *AUTOAMERICAN* ~ 997 points

Rank/Album/Points

4 *THE HUNTER* ~ 644 points

5 *THE BEST OF BLONDIE* ~ 634 points

6. *NO EXIT* ~ 620 points
7. *POLLINATOR* ~ 423 points
8. *THE COMPLETE PICTURE* ~ 382 points
9. *PLASTIC LETTERS* ~ 380 points
10. *KOOKOO* ~ 374 points

11. *DEF DUMB & BLONDE* ~ 261 points
12. *GREATEST HITS* ~ 260 points
13. *ATOMIC – THE VERY BEST OF* ~ 237 points
14. *AGAINST THE ODDS 1974-1982* ~ 209 points
15. *ROCKBIRD* ~ 152 points

Blondie take the Top 4 places with studio albums, with *PARALLEL LINES* emerging as the band's most successful release, ahead of *EAT TO THE BEAT* and *AUTOAMERICAN*. *THE HUNTER* and the compilation *THE BEST OF BLONDIE* round off the Top 5.

Solo, Debbie's most successful album is her debut, *KOOKOO*, which is ranked at no.10, one place but more than a hundred points ahead of her *DEF DUMB & BLONDE* album.

The most recent release to make the Top 15 is the 2022 box-set, *AGAINST THE ODDS 1974-1982*, which ranks at no.14.

EVENT

THE MAIL ON SUNDAY

Debbie Harry
BLONDIE on BLONDIE

How I survived heroin, a serial killer and losing all my money – to play Glastonbury... at 68

PLUS
SUMMER
FOOD & DRINK
SPECIAL
TOM PARKER BOWLES' hot picnics
& OLLY SMITH'S cool drinks

ALBUMS TRIVIA

To date, Blondie has achieved 17 Top 40 albums, including one compilation also credited to Deborah Harry, who has achieved four solo Top 40 albums.

There follows a country-by-country look at Blondie's and Debbie/Deborah Harry's most successful albums.

BLONDIE & DEBORAH HARRY IN AUSTRALIA

Most Hits

14 hits	Blondie
5 hits	Deborah Harry

Most Weeks

221 weeks	Blondie
75 weeks	Deborah Harry

Note: the number of weeks *NO EXIT* spent on the chart is not known.

No.1 Albums

1981   *THE BEST OF BLONDIE*

THE BEST OF BLONDIE topped the chart for two weeks.

Albums with the most weeks

52 weeks	*EAT TO THE BEAT*
33 weeks	*PARALLEL LINES*
30 weeks	*AUTOAMERICAN*
25 weeks	*DEF DUMB & BLONDE*
24 weeks	*BLONDIE*
23 weeks	*THE BEST OF*
19 weeks	*THE COMPLETE PICTURE*
15 weeks	*PLASTIC LETTERS*
13 weeks	*THE HUNTER*
12 weeks	*ROCKBIRD*

BLONDIE IN AUSTRIA

Blondie achieved five hit albums in Austria, which spent 31 weeks on the chart.

The band's most successful album in Austria is *AUTOAMERICAN*, which peaked at no.18.

Albums with the most weeks

15 weeks	*NO EXIT*
6 weeks	*AUTOAMERICAN*
4 weeks	*PARALLEL LINES*
4 weeks	*EAT TO THE BEAT*

BLONDIE IN BEGIUM (Flanders)

Since 1995, Blondie has achieved three hit albums in Belgium (Flanders), which spent four weeks on the chart.

The band's highest charting album in Belgium (Flanders) is *AGAINST THE ODDS 1972-1984*, which peaked at no.40.

BLONDIE IN FINLAND

Blondie achieved four hit albums in Finland, which spent 61 weeks on the chart.

The band's most successful album is *EAT TO THE BEAT*, which peaked at no.3.

Albums with the most weeks

30 weeks	*PARALLEL LINES*
18 weeks	*EAT TO THE BEAT*
12 weeks	*AUTOAMERICAN*

BLONDIE & DEBORAH HARRY IN FRANCE

Blondie achieved two hit albums in France, which spent nine weeks on the chart.

The band's most successful album is *NO EXIT*, which peaked at no.25 and spent eight weeks on the chart.

BLONDIE IN GERMANY

Blondie have achieved nine hit albums in Germany, which spent 78 weeks on the chart.

The band's most successful album is *PARALLEL LINES*, which peaked at no.9.

Albums with the most weeks

30 weeks	*PARALLEL LINES*
23 weeks	*NO EXIT*
10 weeks	*AUTOAMERICAN*

BLONDIE & DEBORAH HARRY IN JAPAN

Blondie achieved five hit albums in Japan, which spent 50 weeks on the chart. Deborah Harry has achieved one hit album, which spent 11 weeks on the chart.

The most successful album in Japan is *AUTOAMERICAN*, which peaked at no.20.

Albums with the most weeks

15 weeks	*AUTOAMERICAN*
12 weeks	*PARALLEL LINES*
11 weeks	*KOOKOO*
9 weeks	*THE BEST OF*
8 weeks	*EAT TO THE BEAT*

BLONDIE IN THE NETHERLANDS

Blondie achieved 12 hit albums in the Netherlands, which spent 74 weeks on the chart.

The band's most successful album is *PLASTIC LETTERS*, which peaked at no.2.

Albums with the most weeks

21 weeks	*PLASTIC LETTERS*
14 weeks	*PARALLEL LINES*
7 weeks	*THE COMPLETE PICTURE*
7 weeks	*NO EXIT*
6 weeks	*EAT TO THE BEAT*

BLONDIE & DEBORAH HARRY IN NEW ZEALAND

Blondie achieved 10 hit albums in New Zealand, which spent 152 weeks on the chart. Deborah Harry has achieved two hit albums (one jointly with Blondie), and has spent 32 weeks on the chart.

No.1 Albums

1981	*THE BEST OF*
1991	*THE COMPLETE PICTURE*

Most weeks at No.1

3 weeks	*THE BEST OF*
2 weeks	*THE COMPLETE PICTURE*

Albums with the most weeks

41 weeks	*PARALLEL LINES*
34 weeks	*EAT TO THE BEAT*
23 weeks	*THE COMPLETE PICTURE*
20 weeks	*AUTOAMERICAN*
12 weeks	*THE BEST OF*

BLONDIE IN NORWAY

Blondie achieved five hit albums in Norway, which spent 64 weeks on the chart.

The band's most successful album is *EAT TO THE BEAT*, which peaked at no.6.

Albums with the most weeks

28 weeks	*EAT TO THE BEAT*
14 weeks	*AUTOAMERICAN*
12 weeks	*THE HUNTER*

BLONDIE IN SPAIN

Blondie has achieved three hit albums in Spain, which spent 13 weeks on the chart.

The band's most successful album is *PARALLEL LINES*, which peaked at no.24.

Albums with the most weeks

9 weeks   *PARALLEL LINES*
3 weeks   *GREATEST HITS: SOUND & VISION*

BLONDIE & DEBORAH HARRY IN SWEDEN

Most Hits

7 hits   Blondie
2 hits   Deborah Harry

Most Weeks

114 weeks   Blondie
16 weeks   Deborah Harry

The most successful album in Sweden is *EAT TO THE BEAT*, which peaked at no.2.

Albums with the most weeks

54 weeks   *PARALLET LINES*
20 weeks   *EAT TO THE BEAT*
14 weeks   *AUTOAMERICAN*
10 weeks   *NO EXIT*
10 weeks   *KOOKOO*

BLONDIE IN SWITZERLAND

Only three Blondie albums have charted in Switzerland, which spent 21 weeks on the chart.

The highest charting album is *NO EXIT*, which peaked at no.21.

Albums with the most weeks

17 weeks   *NO EXIT*
3 weeks   *POLLINATOR*
1 week   *AGAINST THE ODDS 1974-1982*

BLONDIE & DEBORAH HARRY IN THE UK

Most Hits

19 hits Blondie
 6 hits Deborah Harry

Two albums credit both Blondie & Deborah Harry.

Most Weeks

398 weeks Blondie
 44 weeks Deborah Harry

No.1 Albums

1979 *PARALLEL LINES*
1979 *EAT TO THE BEAT*

Most weeks at No.1

4 weeks *PARALLEL LINES*
1 week *EAT TO THE BEAT*

Albums with the most weeks

114 weeks *PARALLEL LINES*
 53 weeks *ATOMIC – THE VERY BEST OF*
 40 weeks *THE BEST OF*
 38 weeks *EAT TO THE BEAT*
 33 weeks *PLASTIC LETTERS*
 23 weeks *THE COMPLETE PICTURE*
 19 weeks *NO EXIT*
 16 weeks *AUTOAMERICAN*
 16 weeks *GREATEST HITS*
 15 weeks *GREATEST HITS (SIGHT & SOUND)*

The BRIT Certified/BPI (British Phonographic Industry) Awards

The BPI began certifying albums in 1973, and between April 1973 and December 1978, awards related to a monetary value and not a unit value. Thanks to inflation, this changed several times over the years:

- April 1973 – August 1974: Silver = £75,000, Gold = £150,000, Platinum = £1 million.
- September 1974 – December 1975: Gold raised to £250,000, others unchanged.
- January 1976 – December 1976: Silver raised to £100,000, others unchanged.
- January 1977 – December 1978: Silver raised to £150,000, Gold raised to £300,000, Platinum unchanged.

When this system was abolished, the awards that were set remain in place today: Silver = 60,000, Gold = 100,000, Platinum = 300,000. Multi-Platinum awards were introduced in February 1987. In July 2013 the BPI automated awards, and awards from this date are based on actual sales since February 1994, not shipments.

2 x Platinum	*THE BEST OF BLONDIE* (August 1988) = 600,000
Platinum	*PARALLEL LINES* (February 1979) = 300,000
Platinum	*EAT TO THE BEAT* (October 1979) = 300,000
Platinum	*AUTOAMERICAN* (December 1980) = 300,000
Platinum	*PLASTIC LETTERS* (August 1981) = 300,000
Platinum	*ATOMIC – GREATEST HITS* (February 1999) = 300,000
Platinum	*GREATEST HITS* (July 2013) = 300,000
Gold	*BLONDIE* (November 1980) = 100,000
Gold	*THE COMPLETE PICTURE* (March 1991) = 100,000
Gold	*NO EXIT* (March 1999) = 100,000
Gold	*PICTURE THIS – THE ESSENTIAL COLLECTION* (July 2013) = 100,000
Gold	*BLONDIE 4(0) EVER* (September 2020) = 100,000
Gold	*THE PLATINUM COLLECTION* (February 2021) = 100,000
Silver	*THE ESSENTIAL COLLECTION* (July 2013) = 60,000
Silver	*DENIS* (July 2013) = 60,000
Silver	*ESSENTIAL* (August 2015) = 60,000

BLONDIE & DEBORAH HARRY IN THE UNITED STATES

Most Hits

8 hits	Blondie
2 hits	Deborah Harry

Most Weeks

165 weeks	Blondie
14 weeks	Deborah Harry

The most successful album in the United States is *PARALLEL LINES*, which peaked at no.6.

Albums with the most weeks

57 weeks	*PARALLEL LINES*
42 weeks	*EAT TO THE BEAT*
28 weeks	*AUTOAMERICAN*
18 weeks	*THE BEST OF*
10 weeks	*KOOKOO*

RIAA (Recording Industry Association of America) Awards

The RIAA began certifying Gold albums in 1958, Platinum albums in 1976, and multi-Platinum albums in 1984. Gold = 500,000, Platinum = 1 million. Awards are based on shipments, not sales, and each disc is counted individually (so, for example, a double album has to ship 500,000 to be eligible for Platinum).

2 x Platinum	*THE BEST OF BLONDIE* (November 2005) = 2 million
Platinum	*PARALLEL LINES* (June 1979) = 1 million
Platinum	*EAT TO THE BEAT* (July 1980) = 1 million
Platinum	*AUTOAMERICAN* (January 1981) = 1 million
Gold	*KOOKOO* (October 1981) = 500,000

BLONDIE IN ZIMBABWE

Blondie achieved two hit albums in Zimbabwe, *PARALLEL LINES* and *THE BEST OF BLONDIE*, which peaked at no.12 and no.11, respectively.

Printed in Great Britain
by Amazon